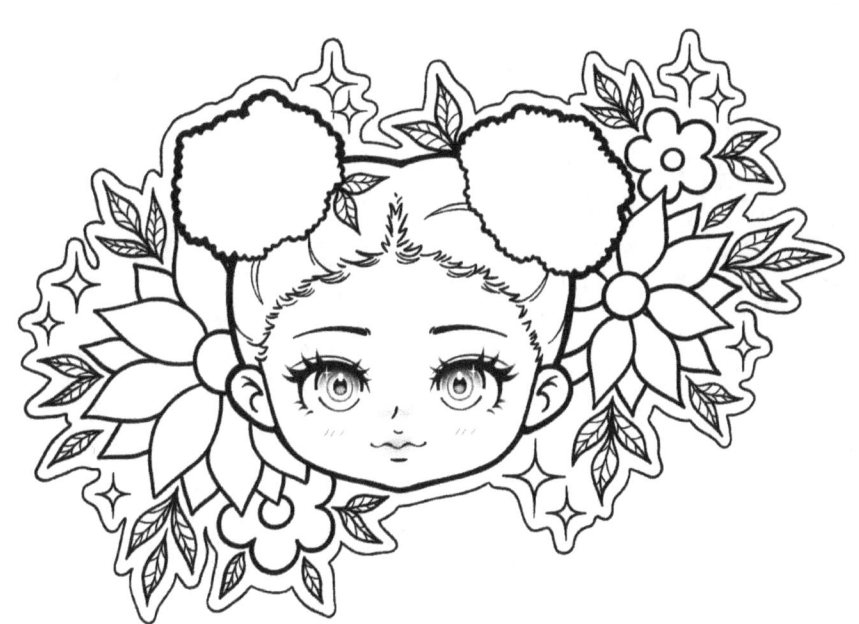

YouTube: www.youtube.com/emzdrawings
Instagram: www.instagram.com/emzdrawings
TikTok: www.tiktok.com/@emzdrawings8

This Book Belongs To:

_____

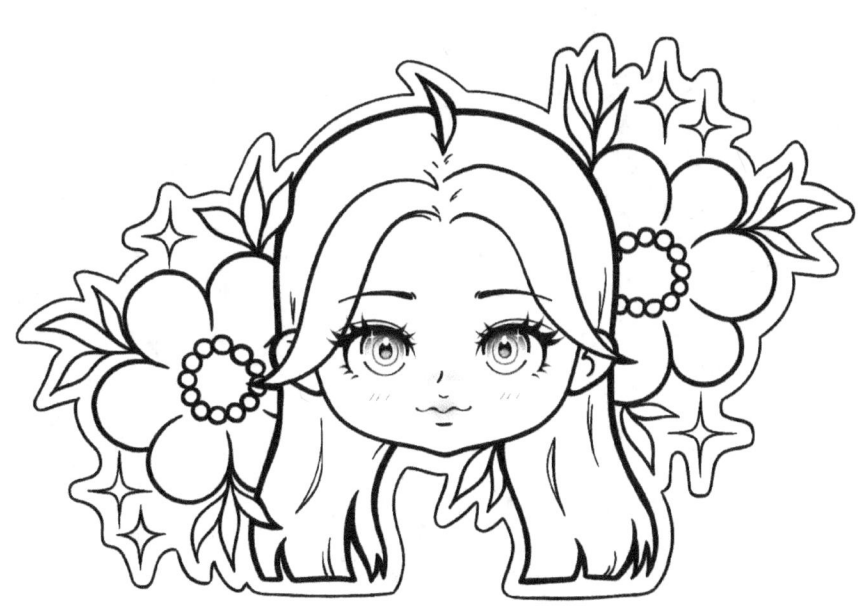

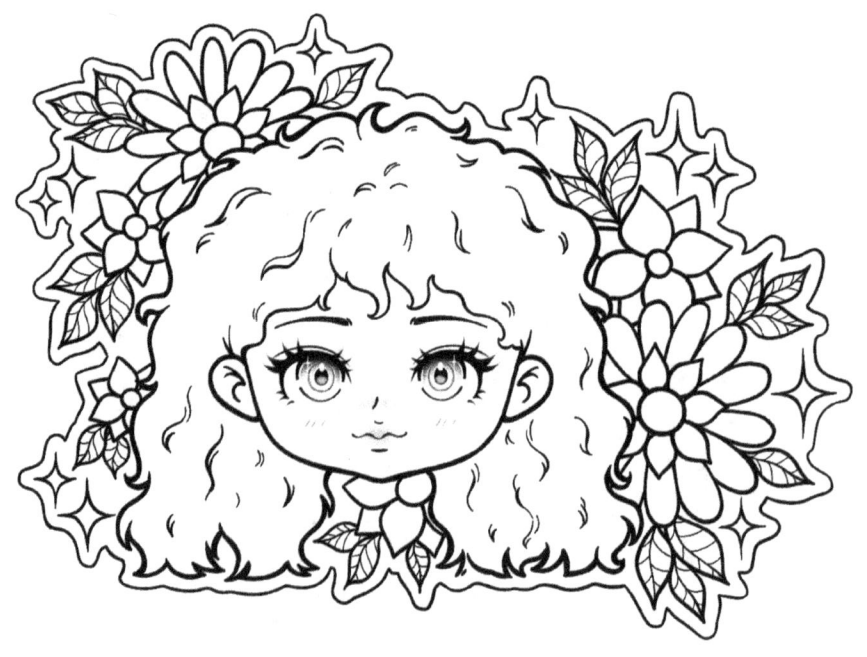

COLORING TIPS

☆ It is recommended to use dry media only in this book

☆ If you're using markers, put a sheet of thick paper behind the page you're coloring to prevent bleed-through to the next page

☆ You can test your colors on the Test Pages at the back of the book

GET MY FREE COLORING BOOK
with 90 original illustrations

Samples:

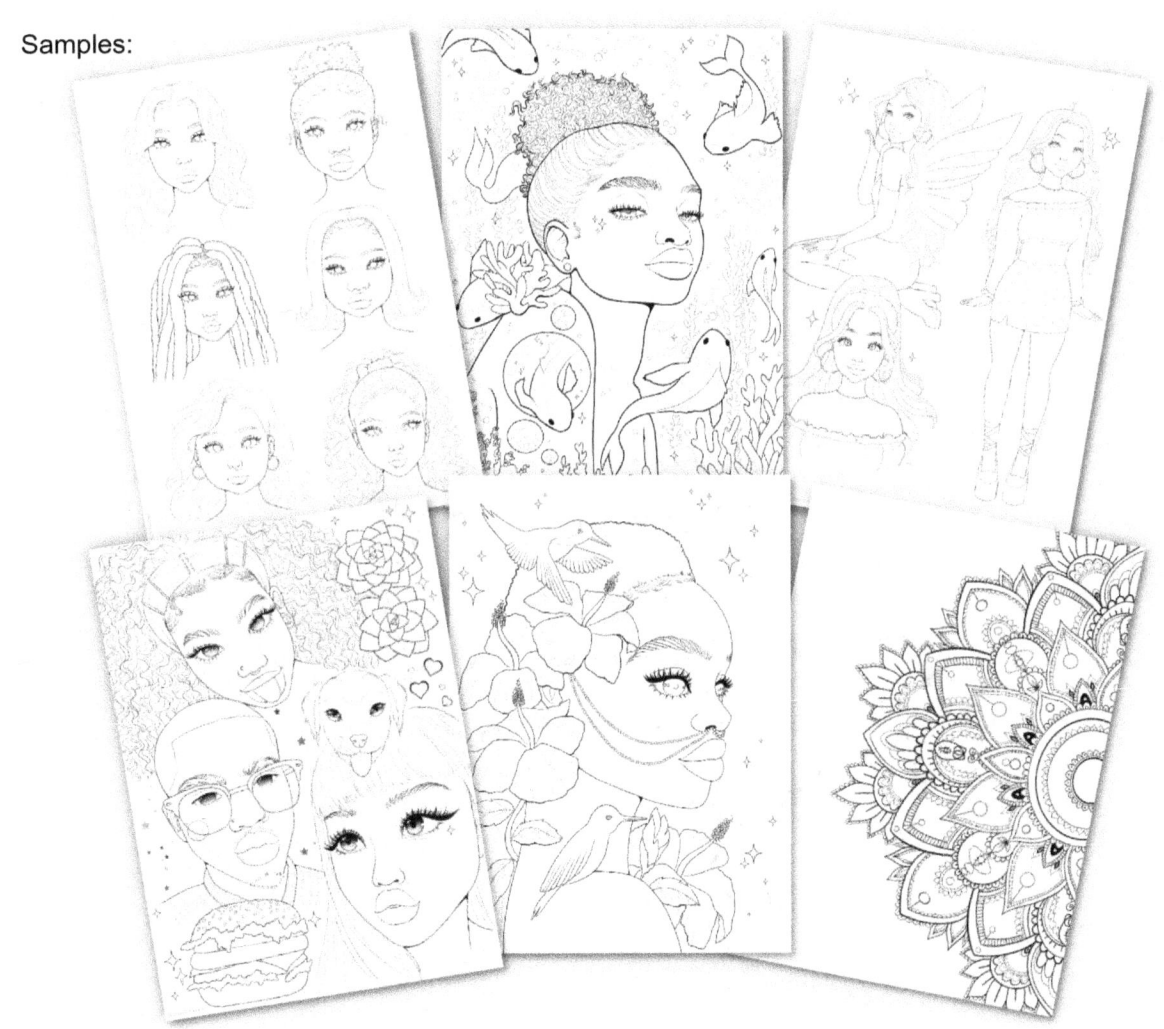

www.emzdrawings.gumroad.com

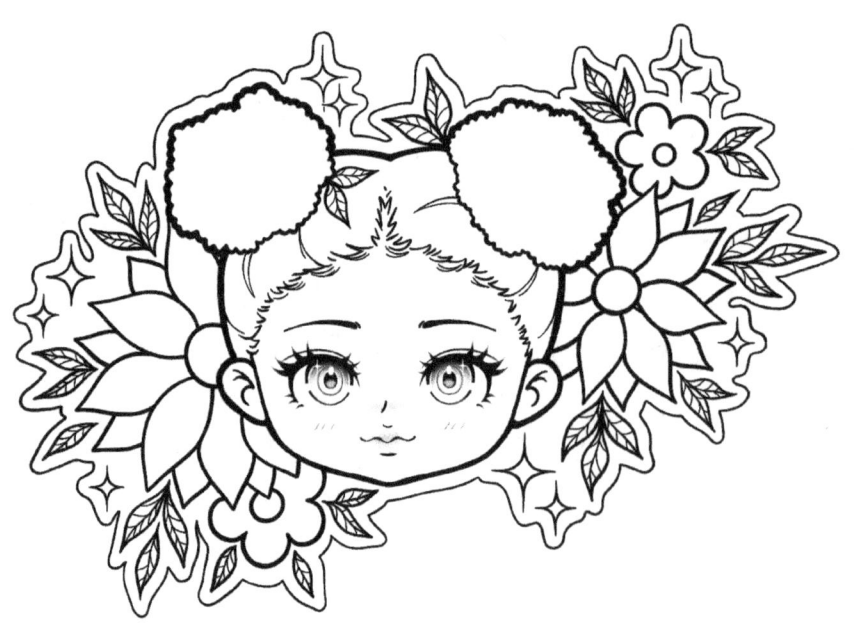

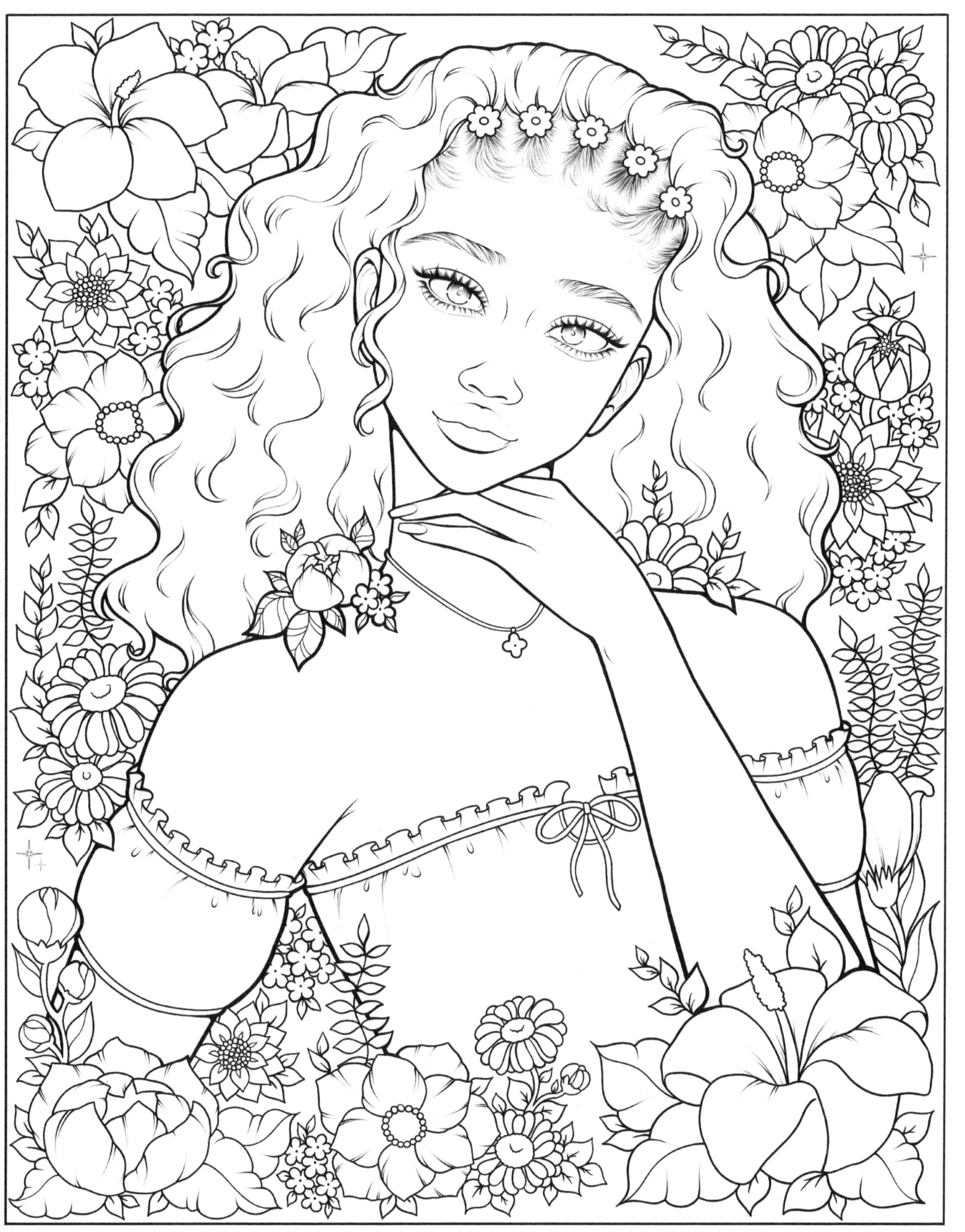

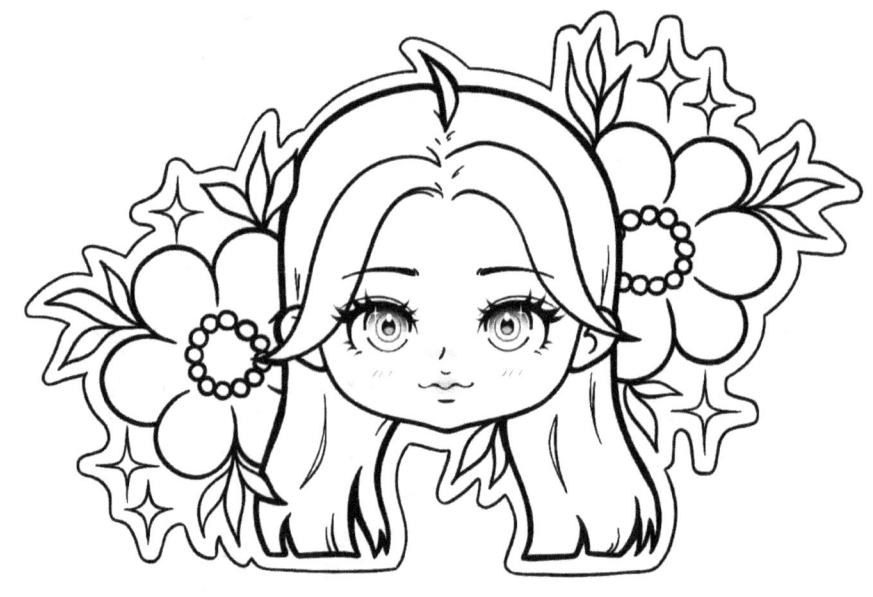

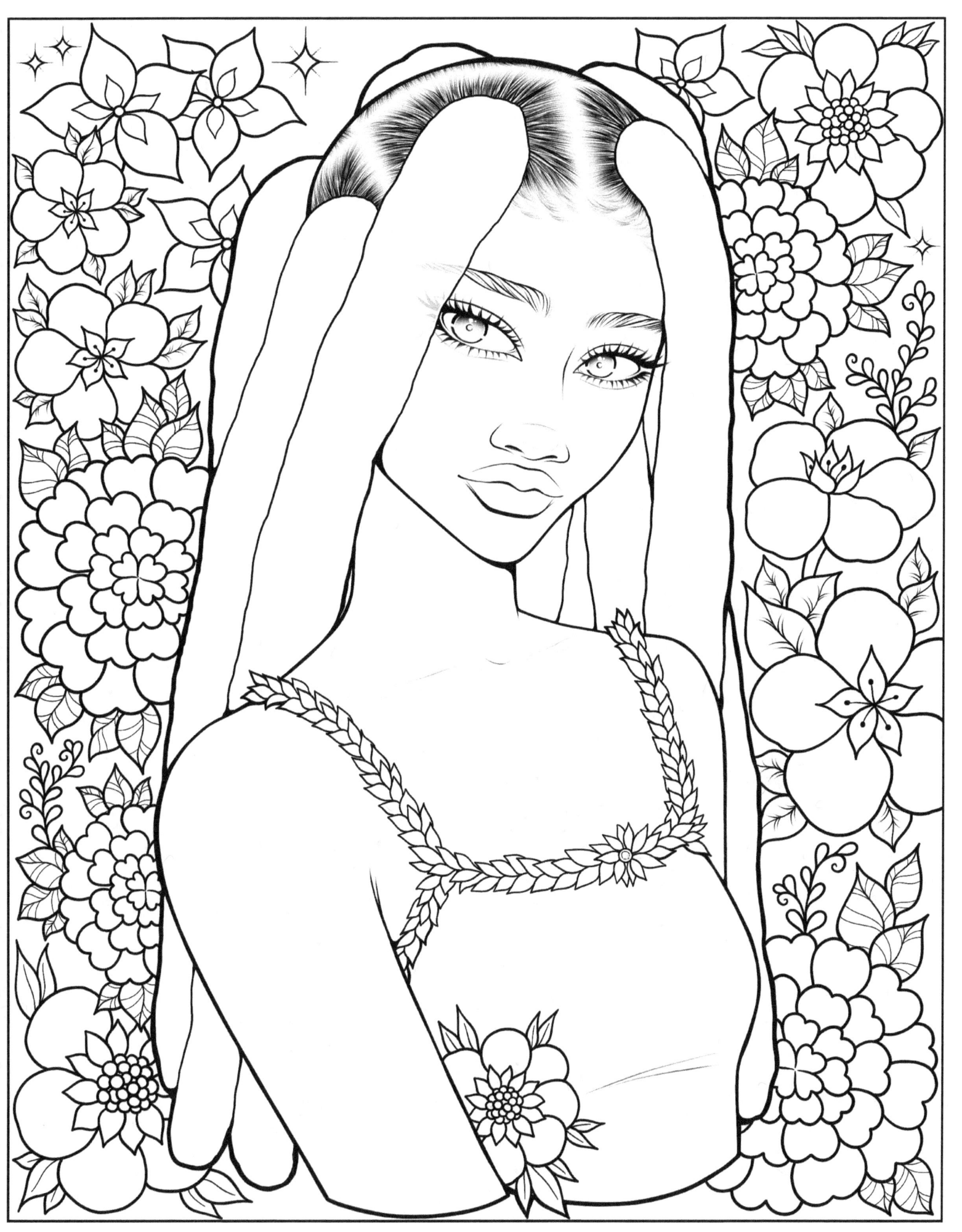

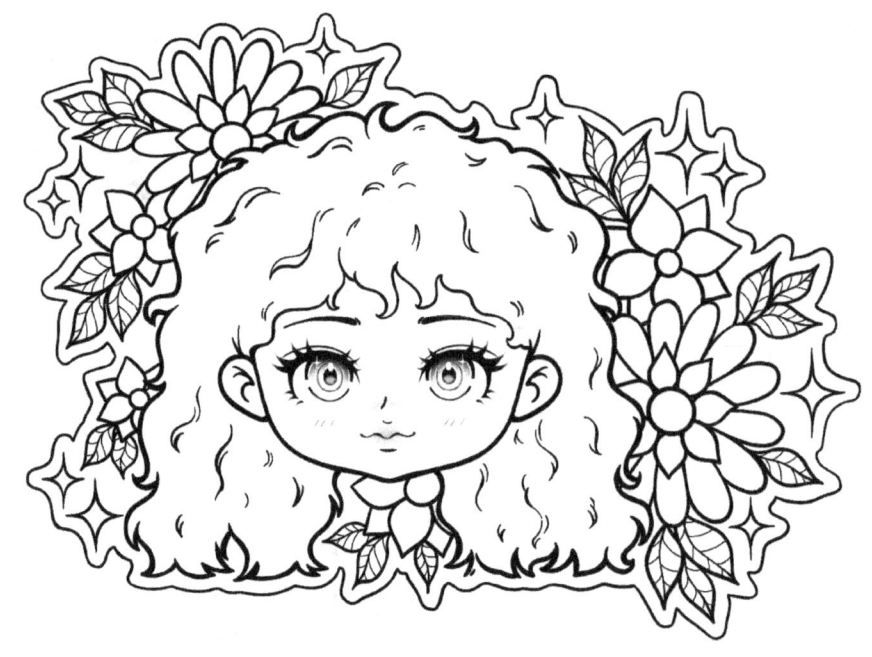

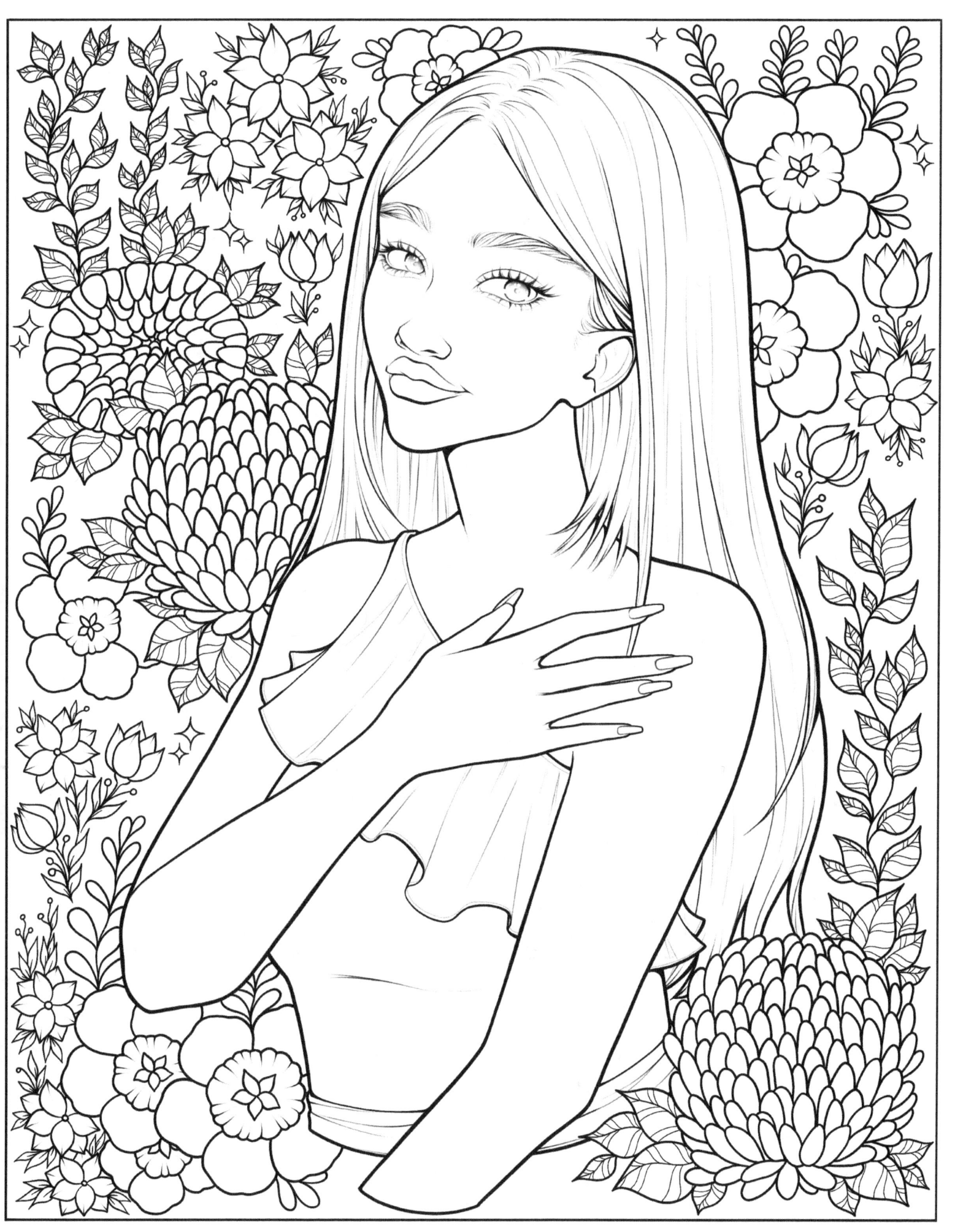

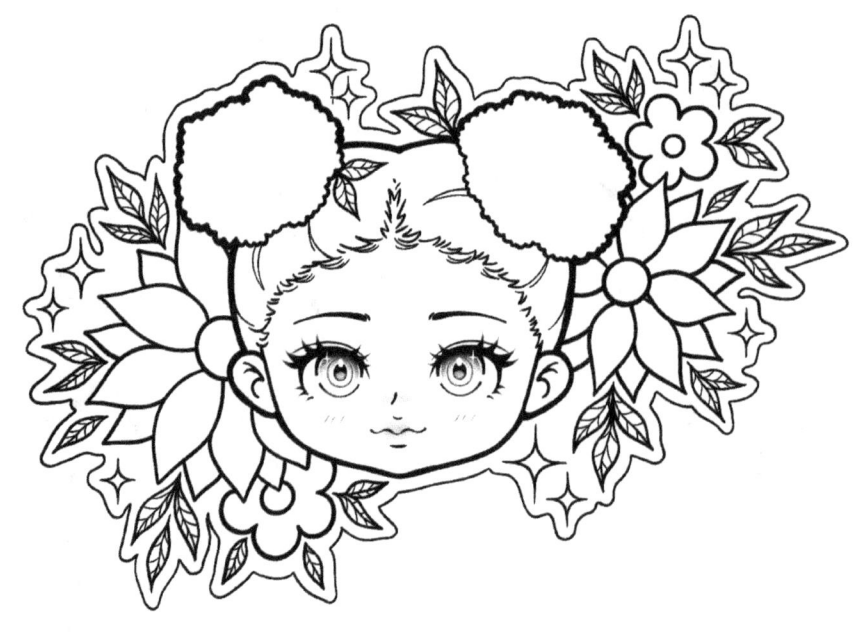

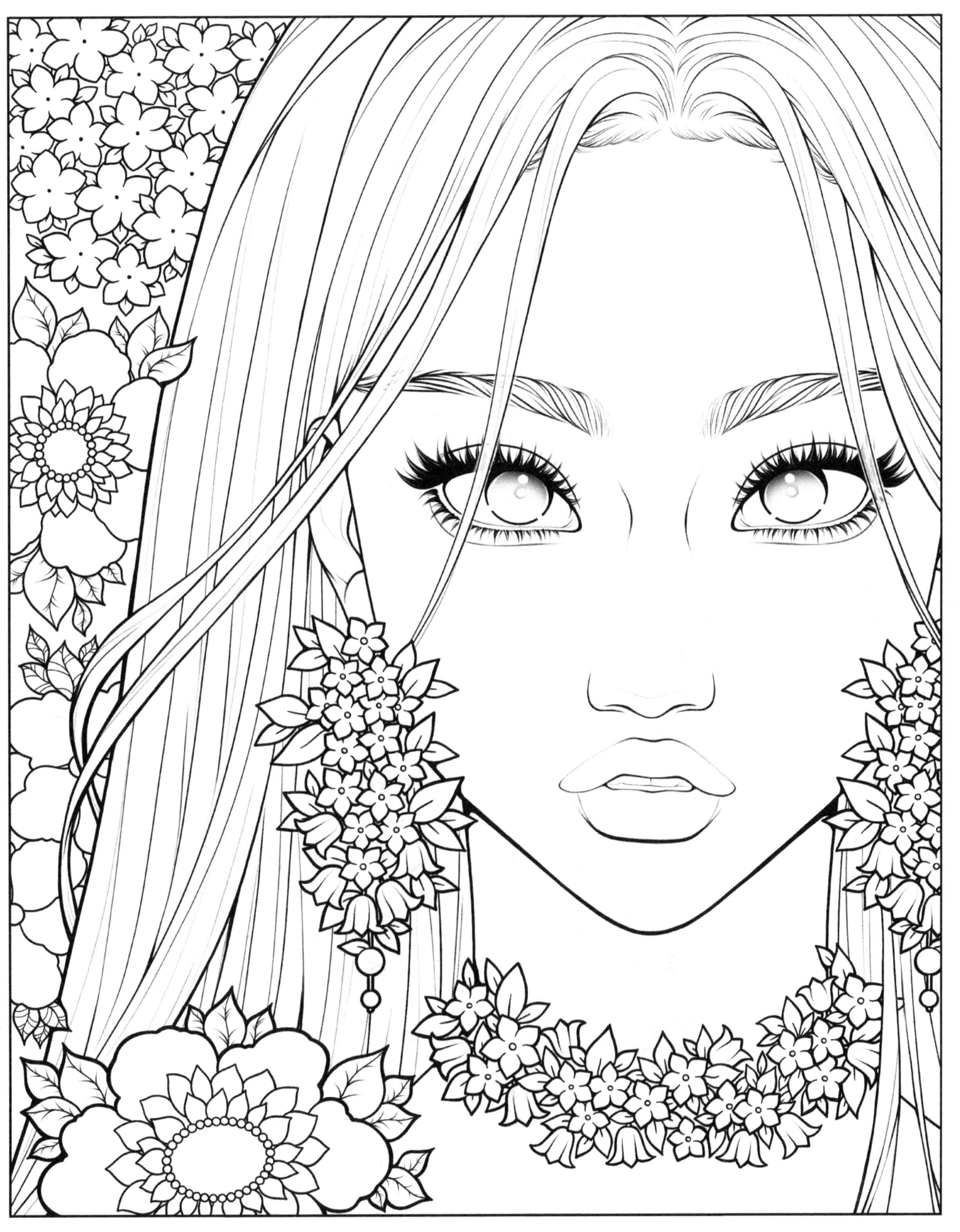

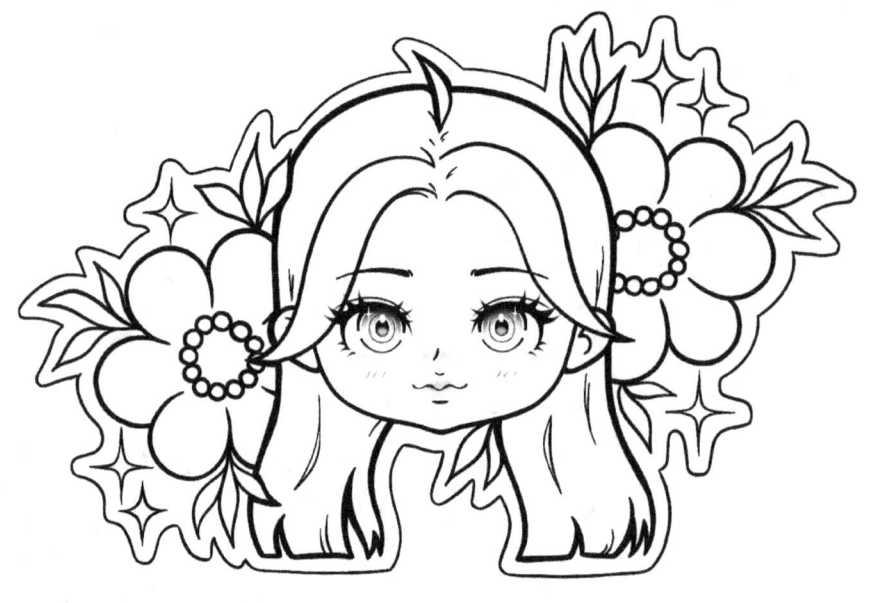

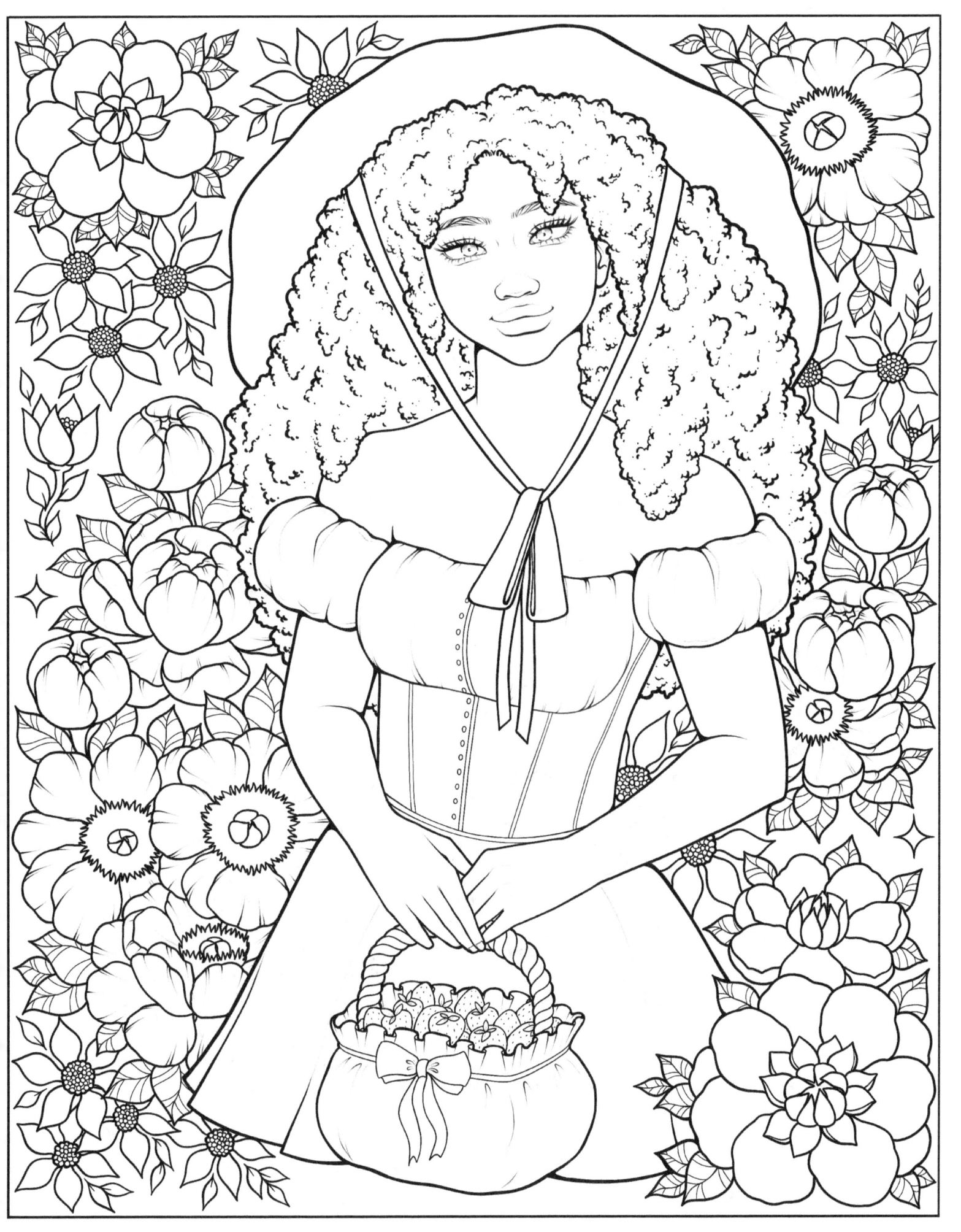

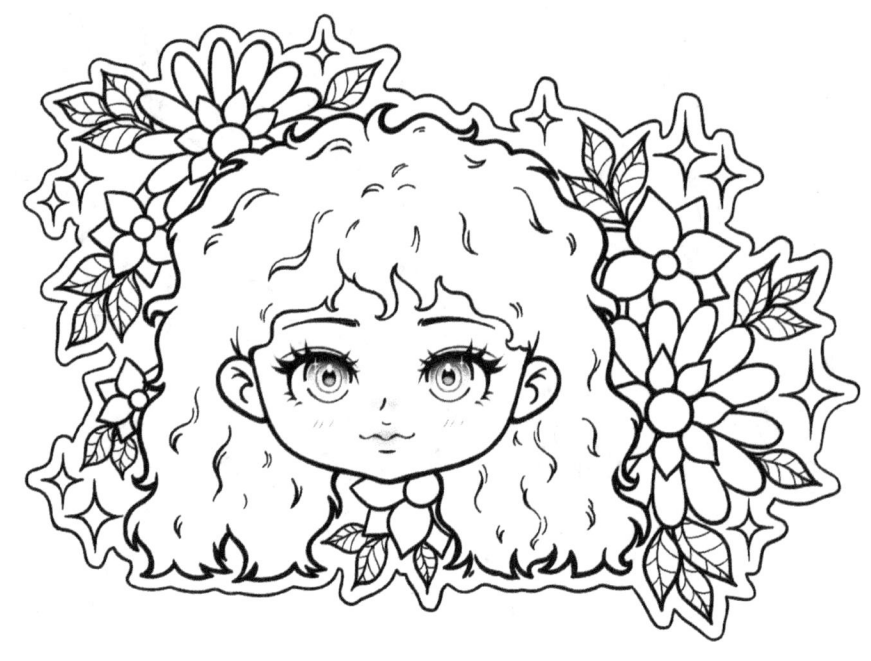

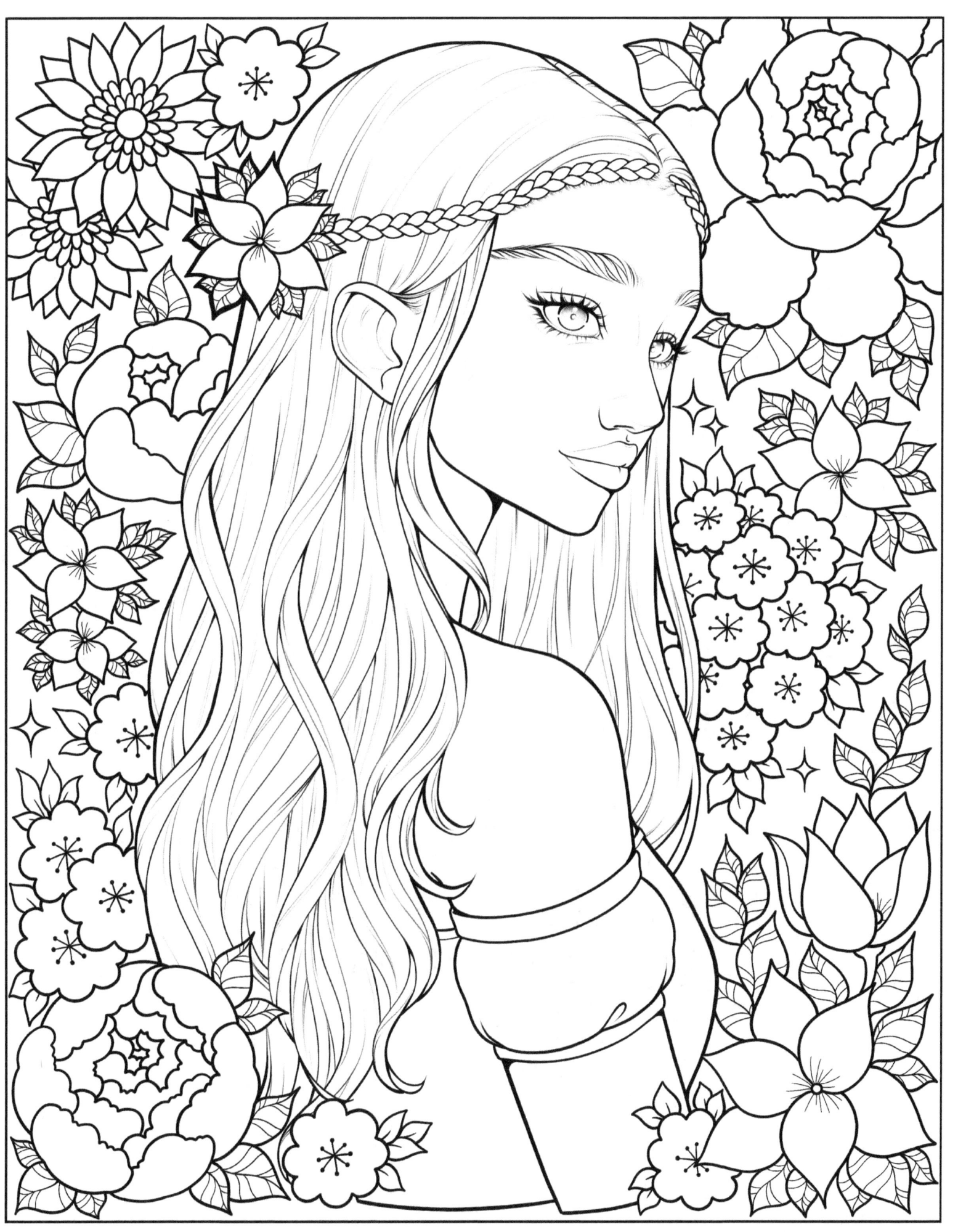

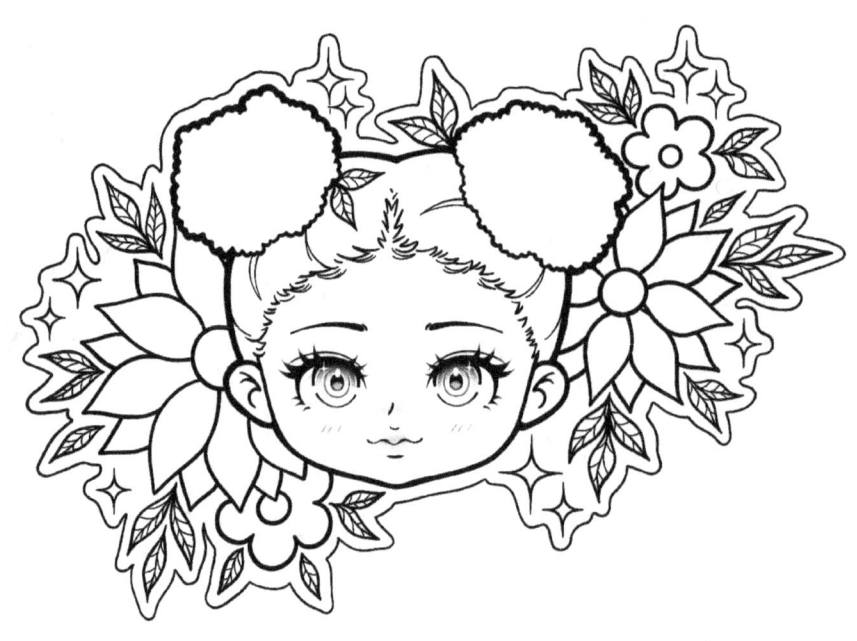

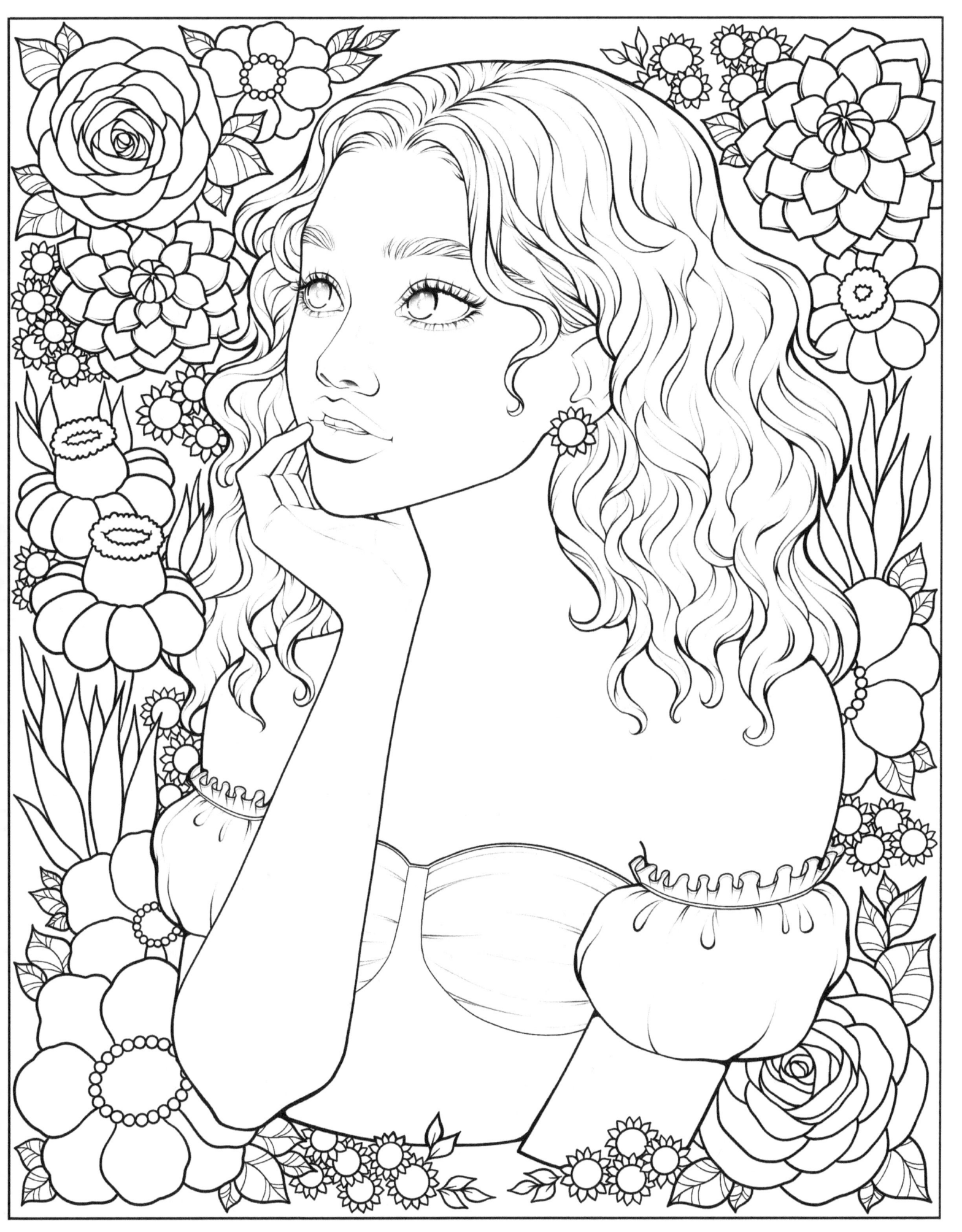

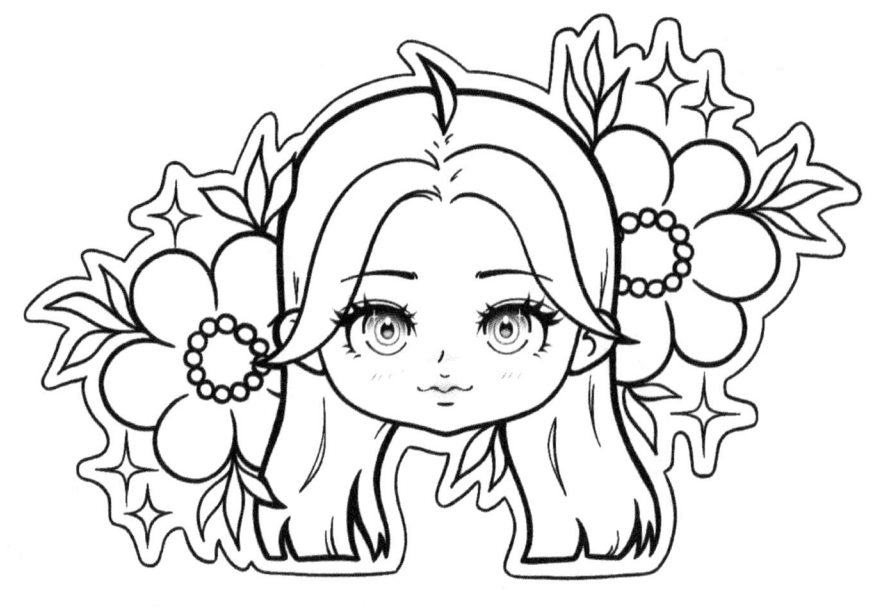

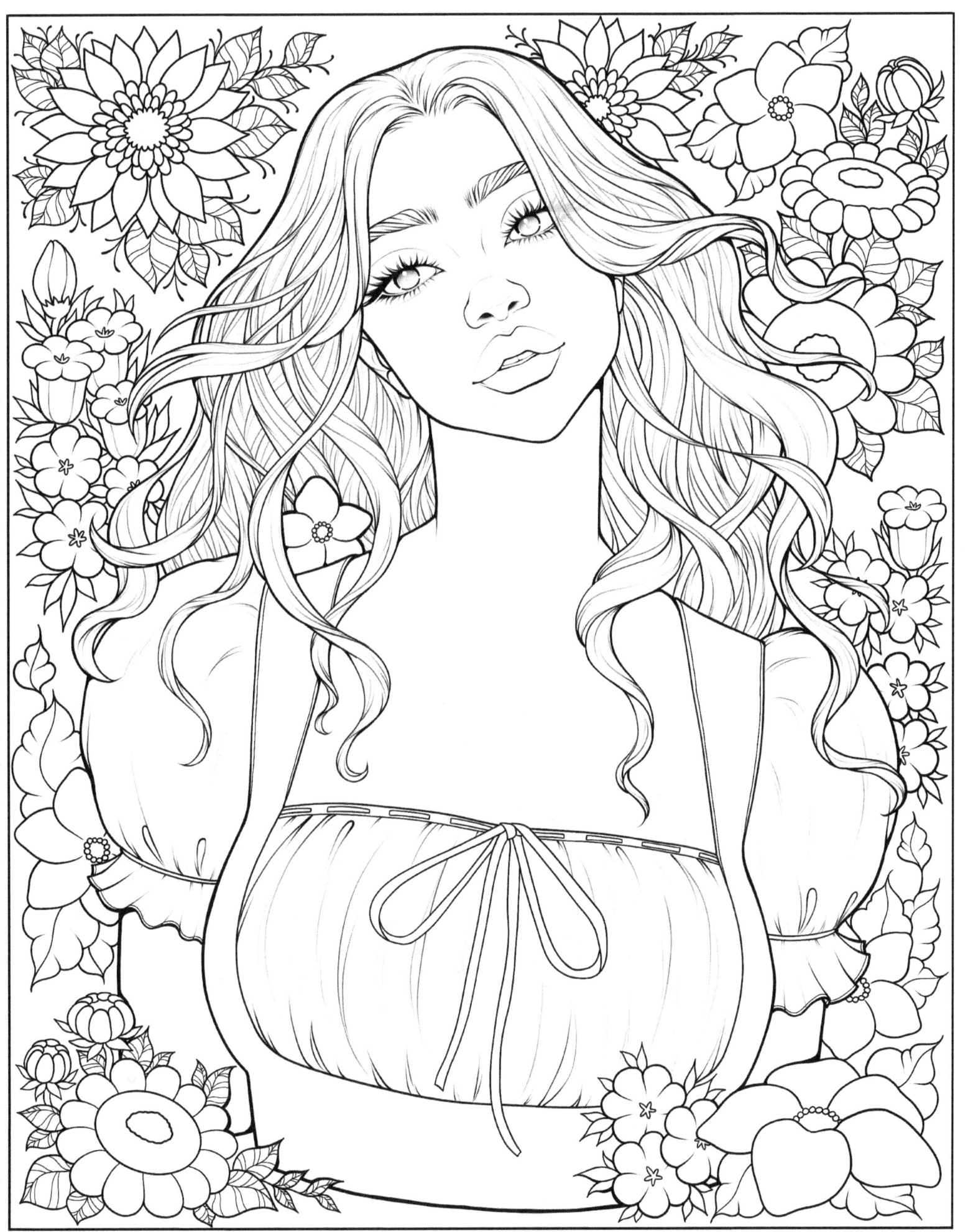

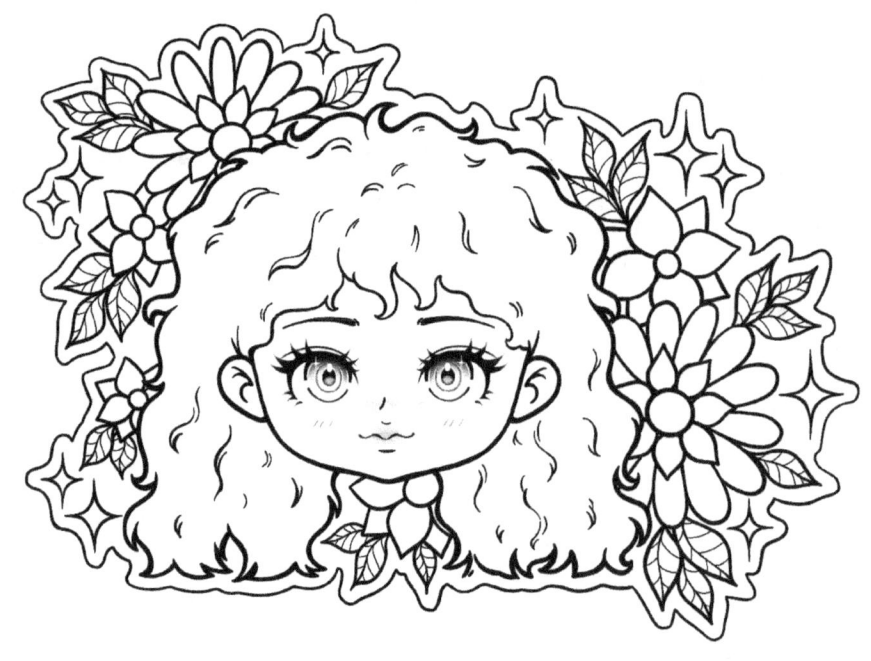

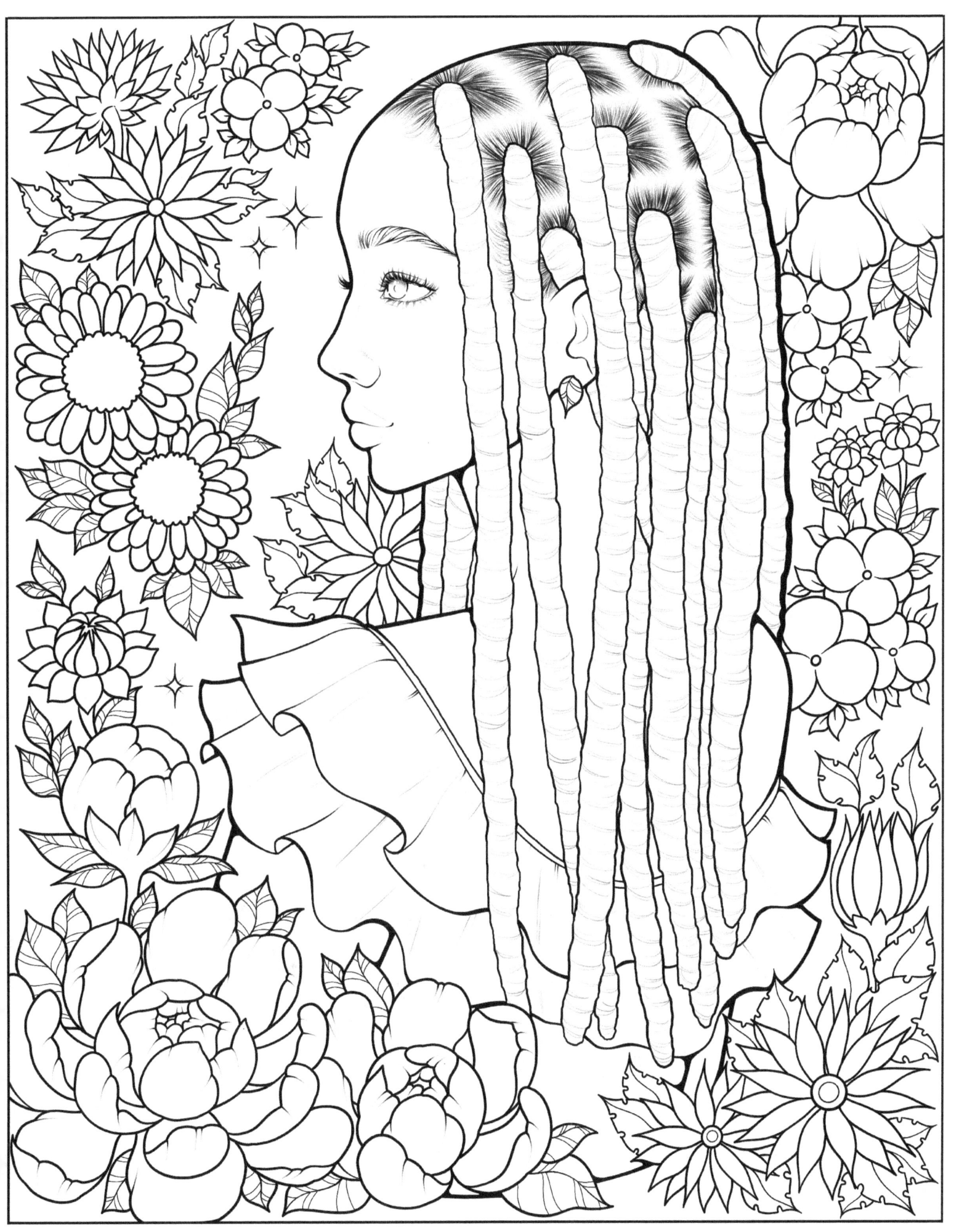

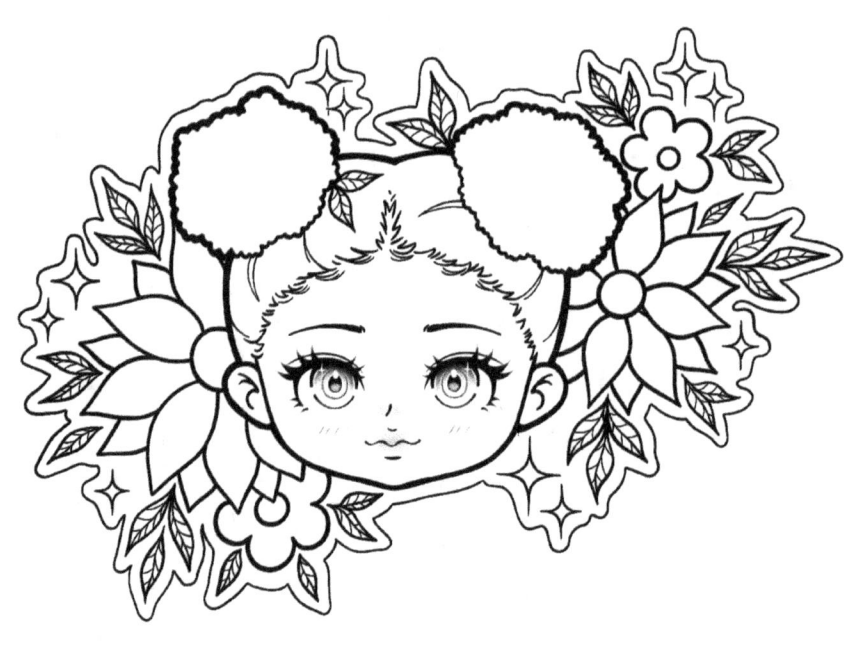

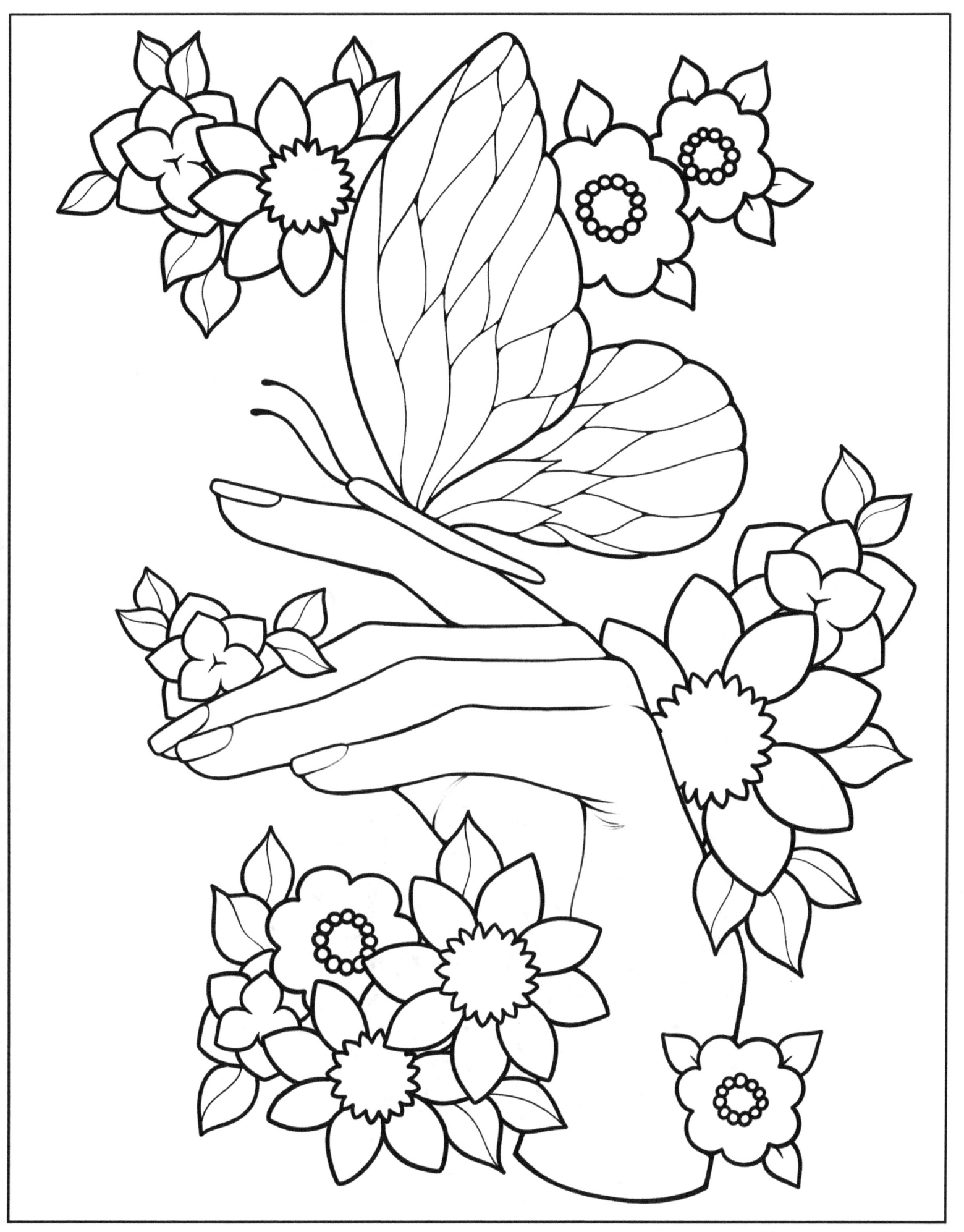

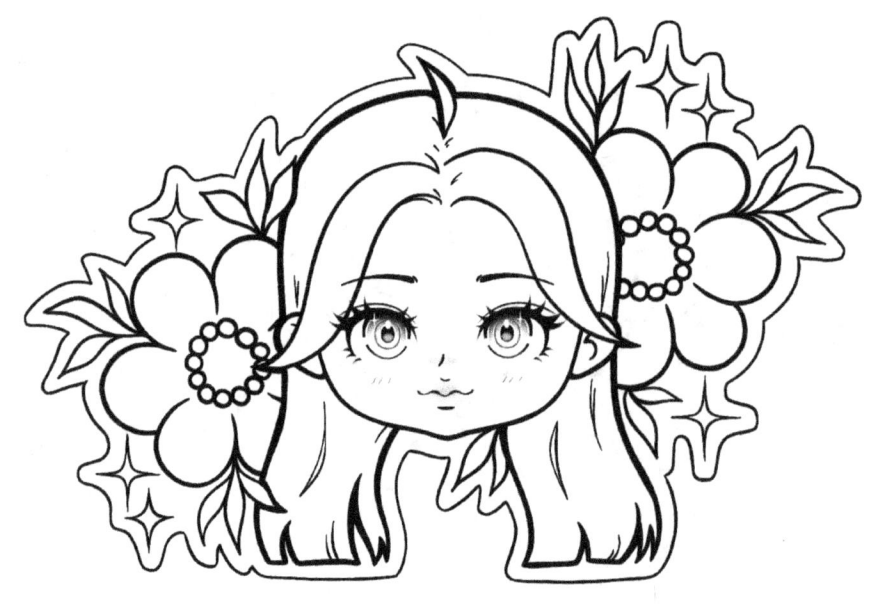

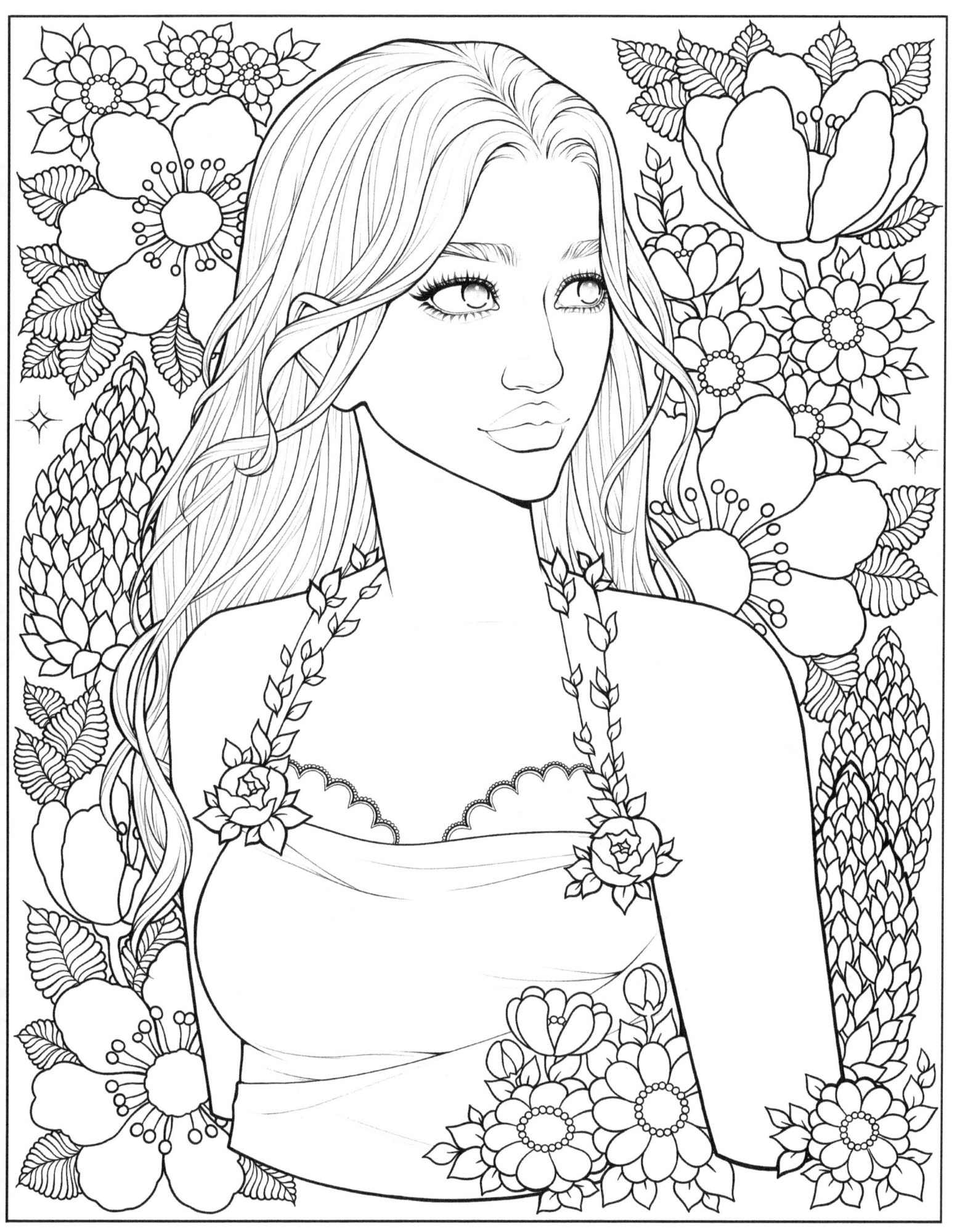

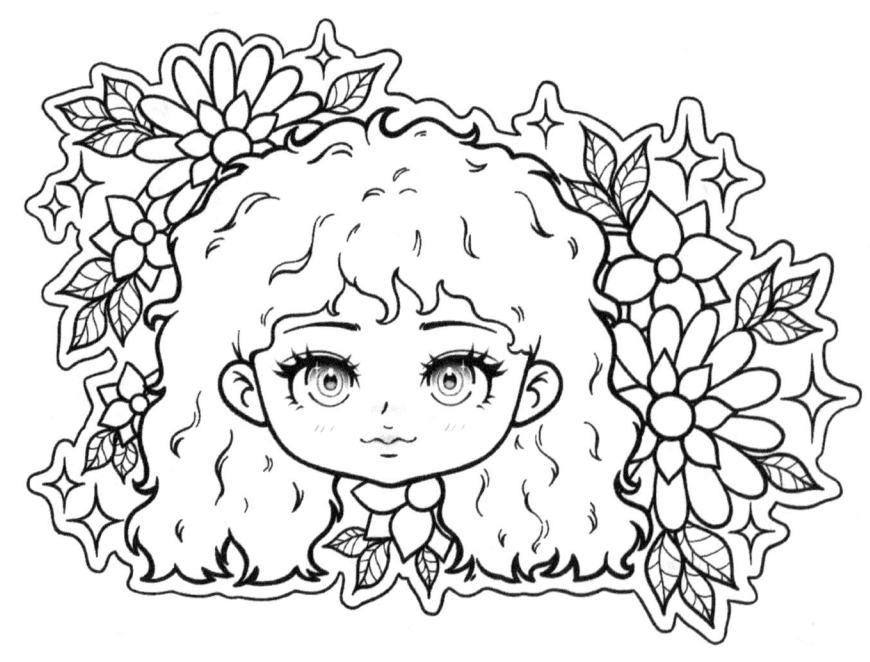

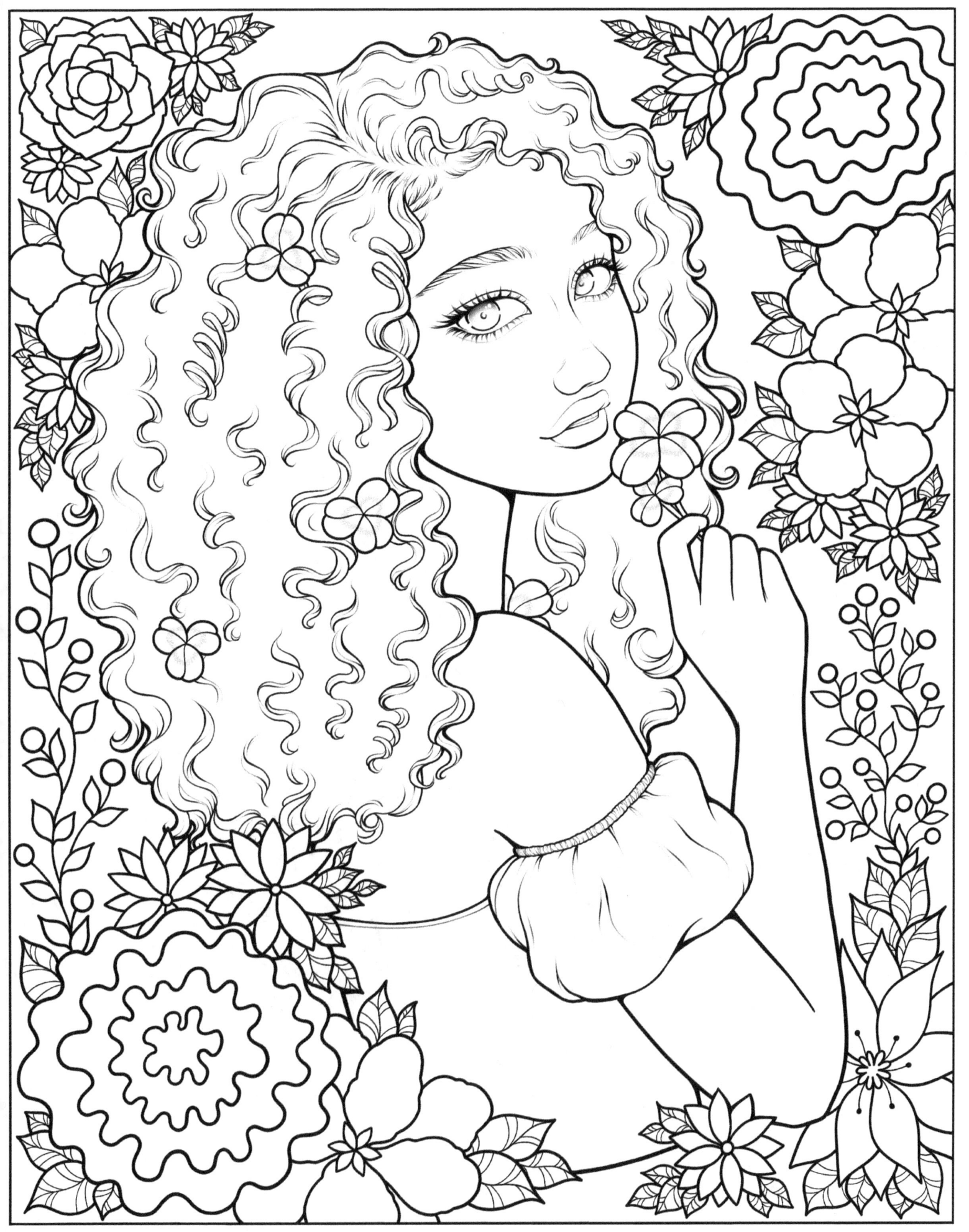

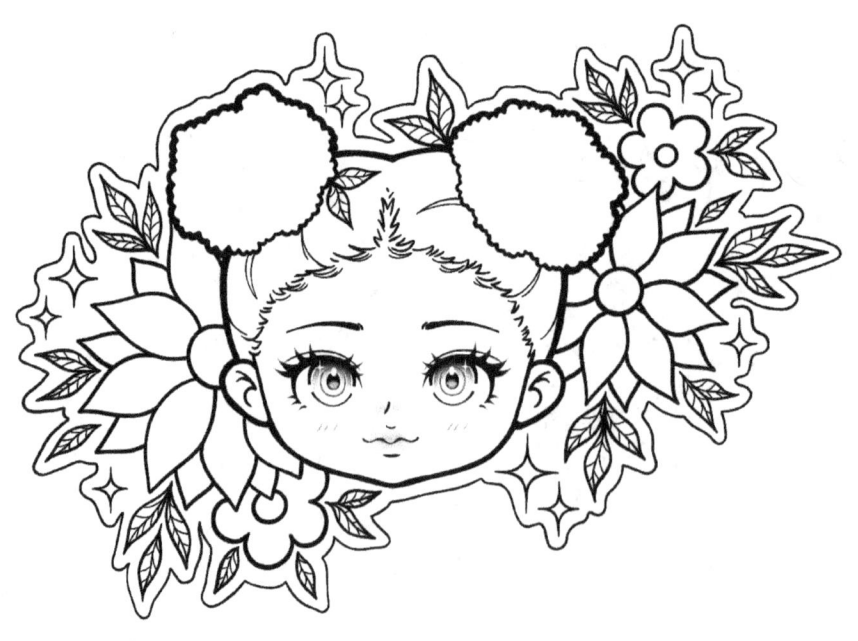

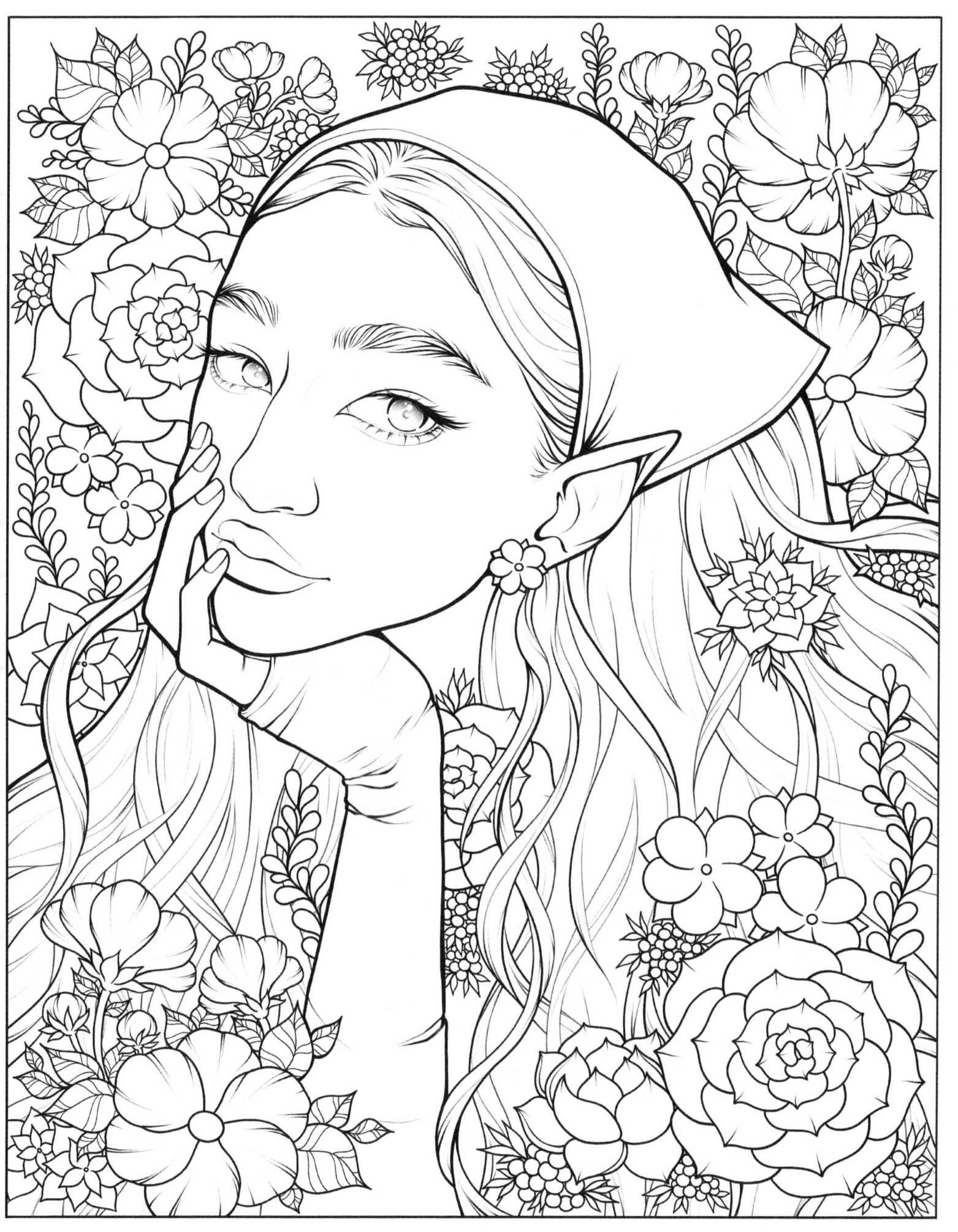

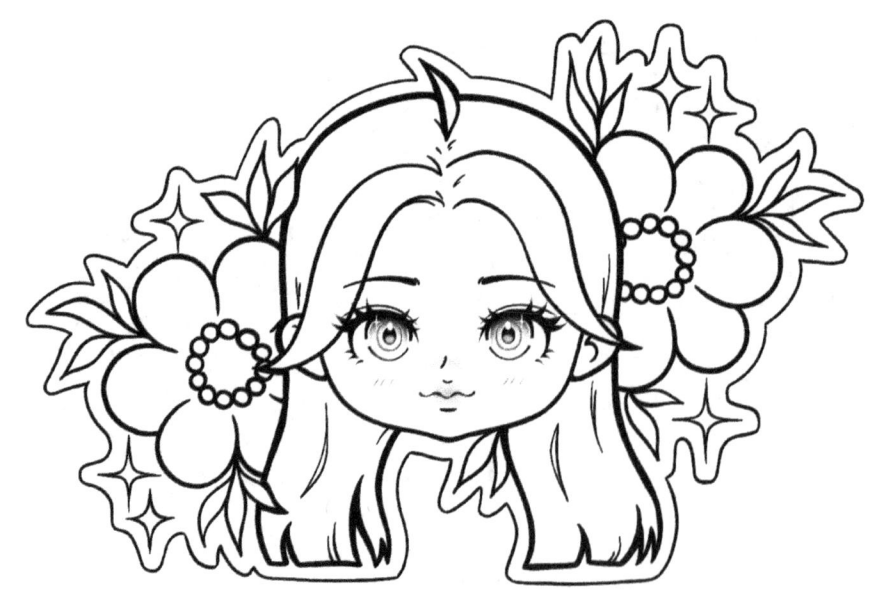

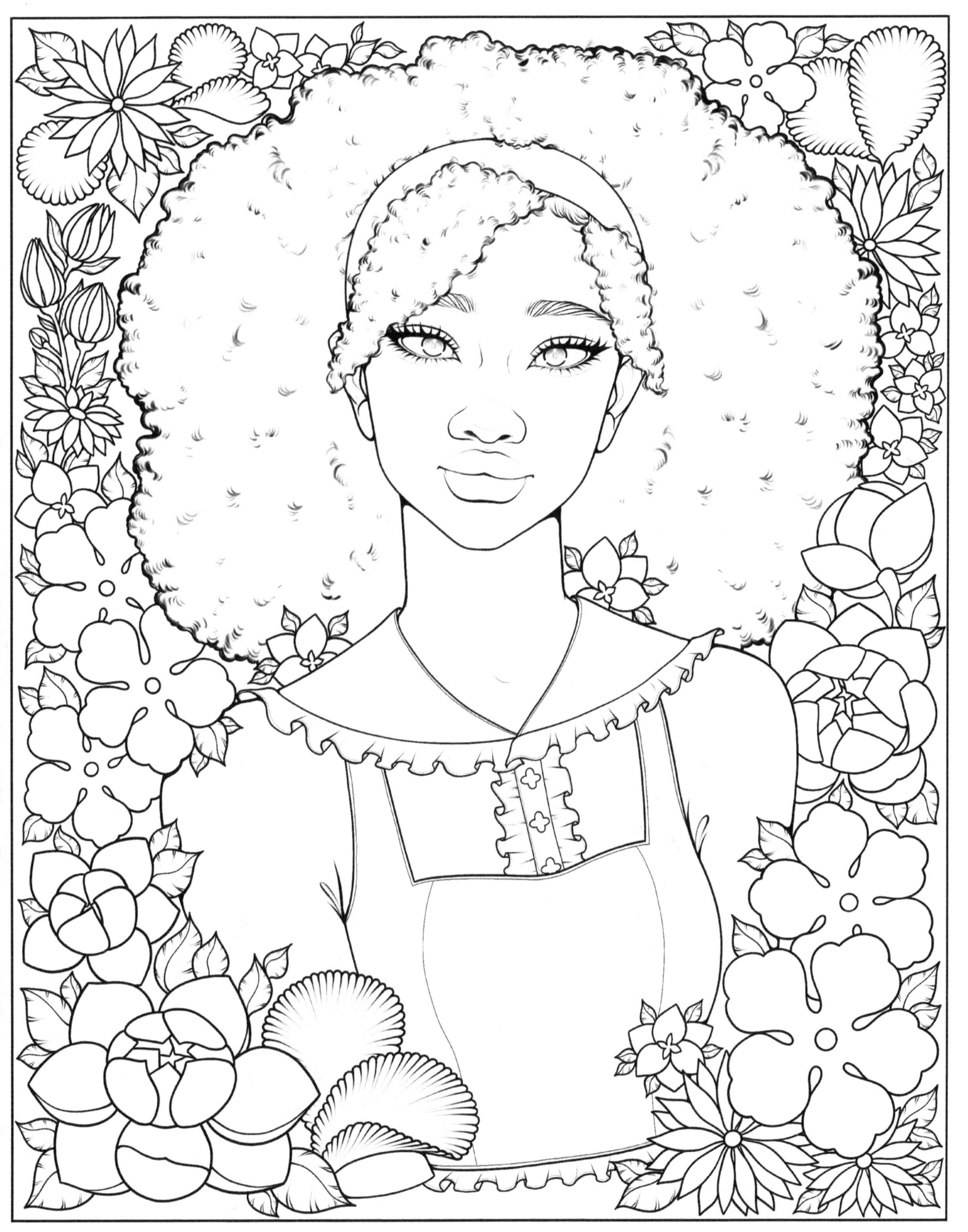

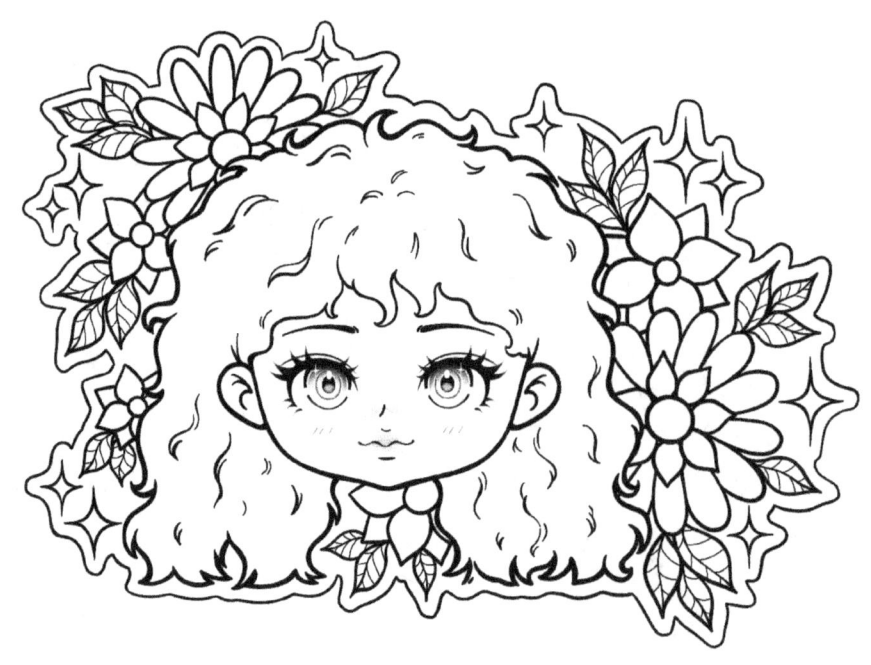

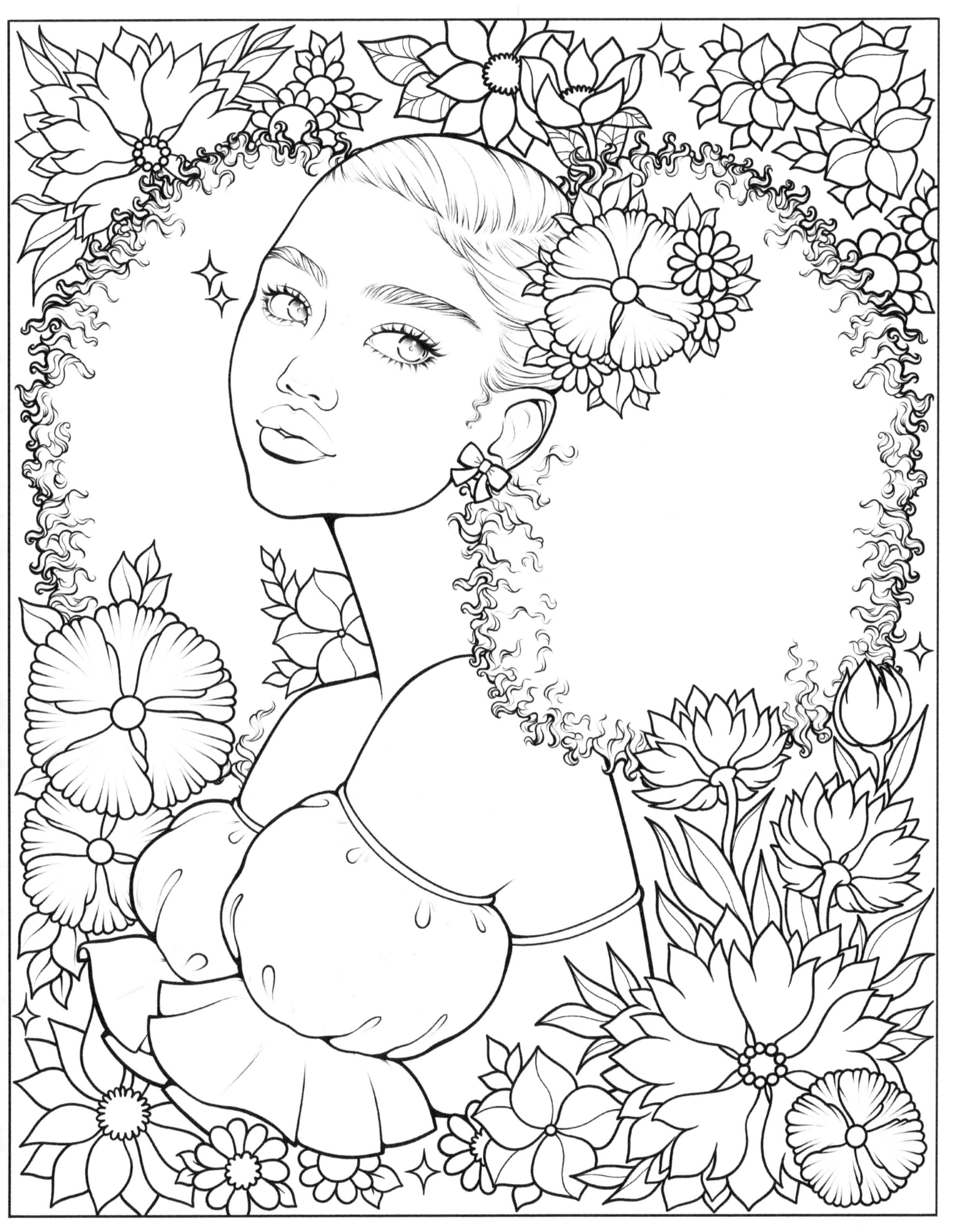

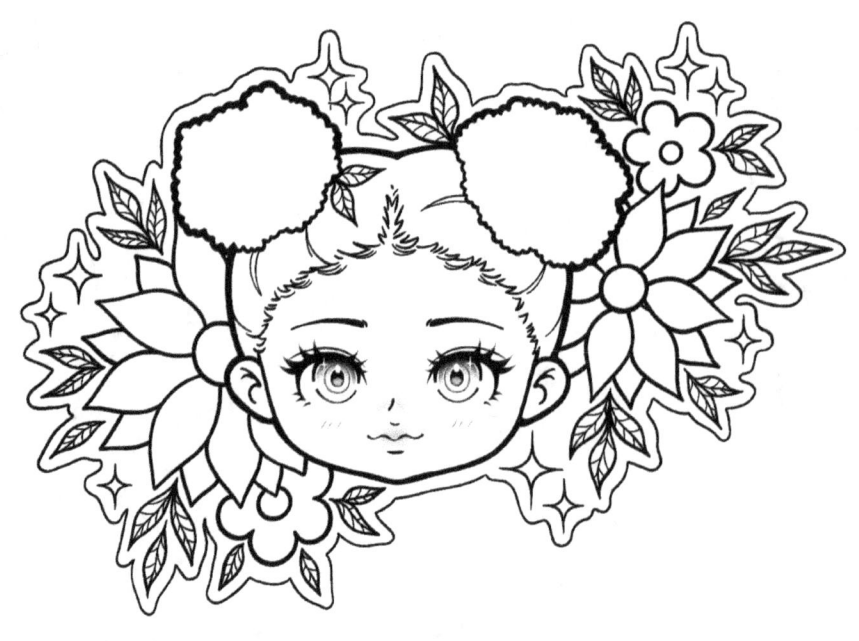

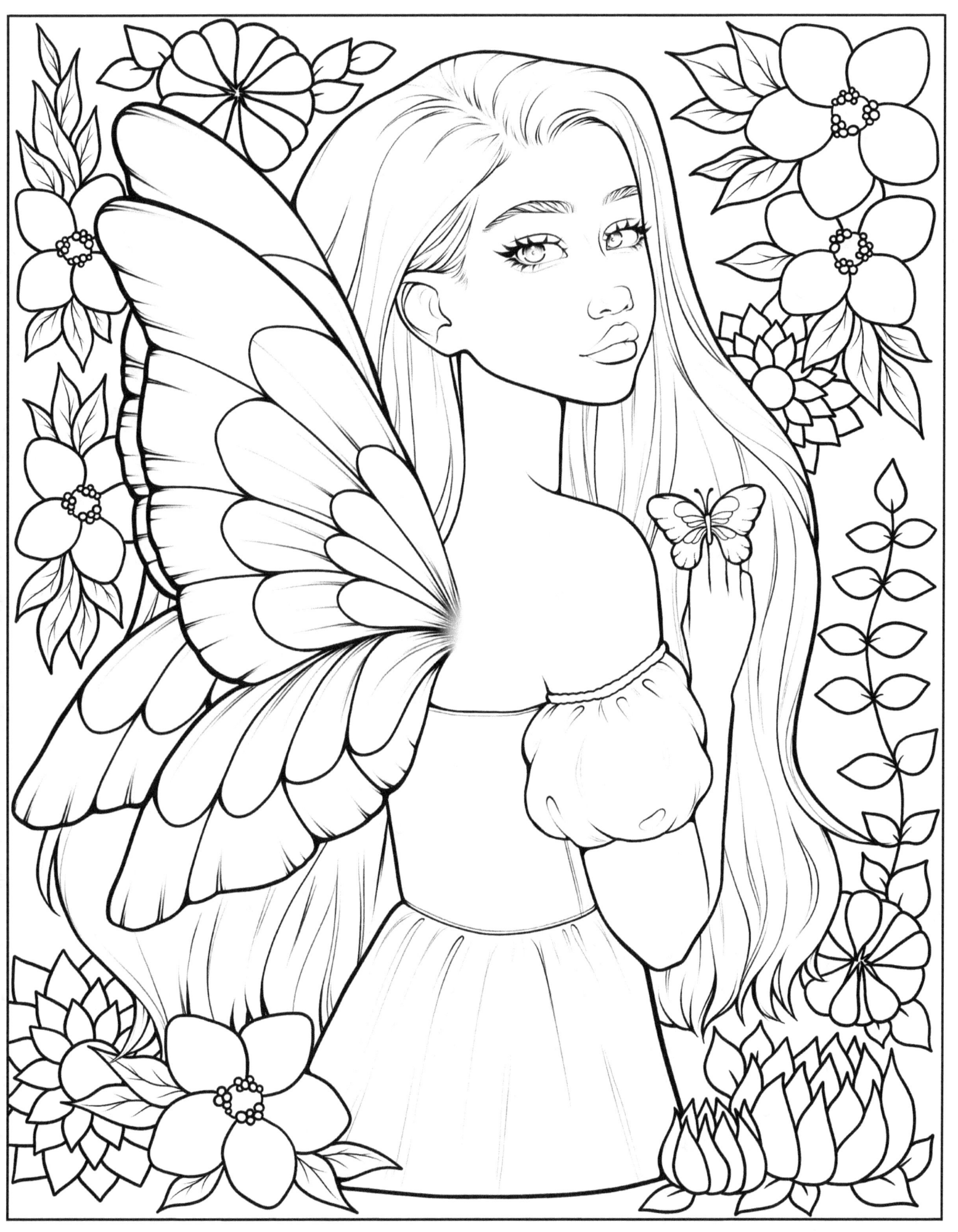

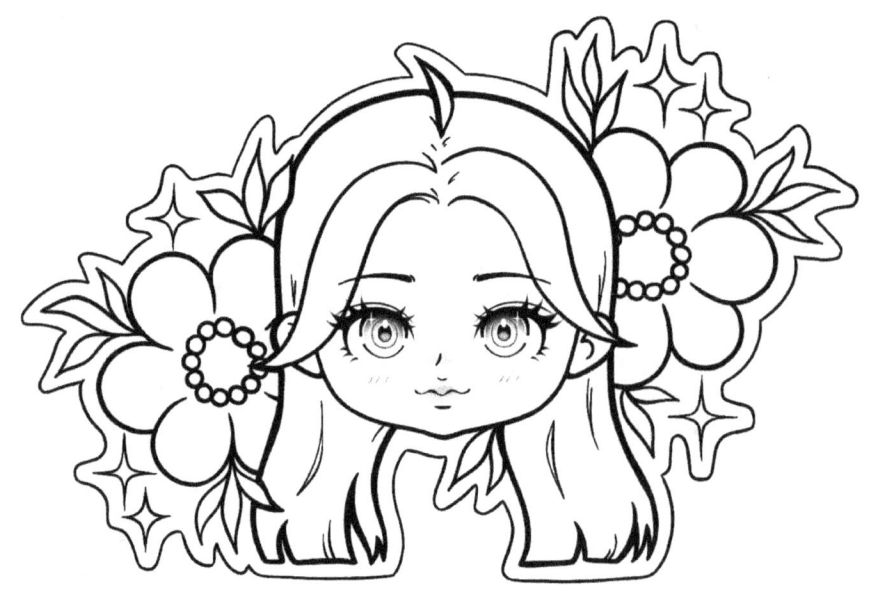

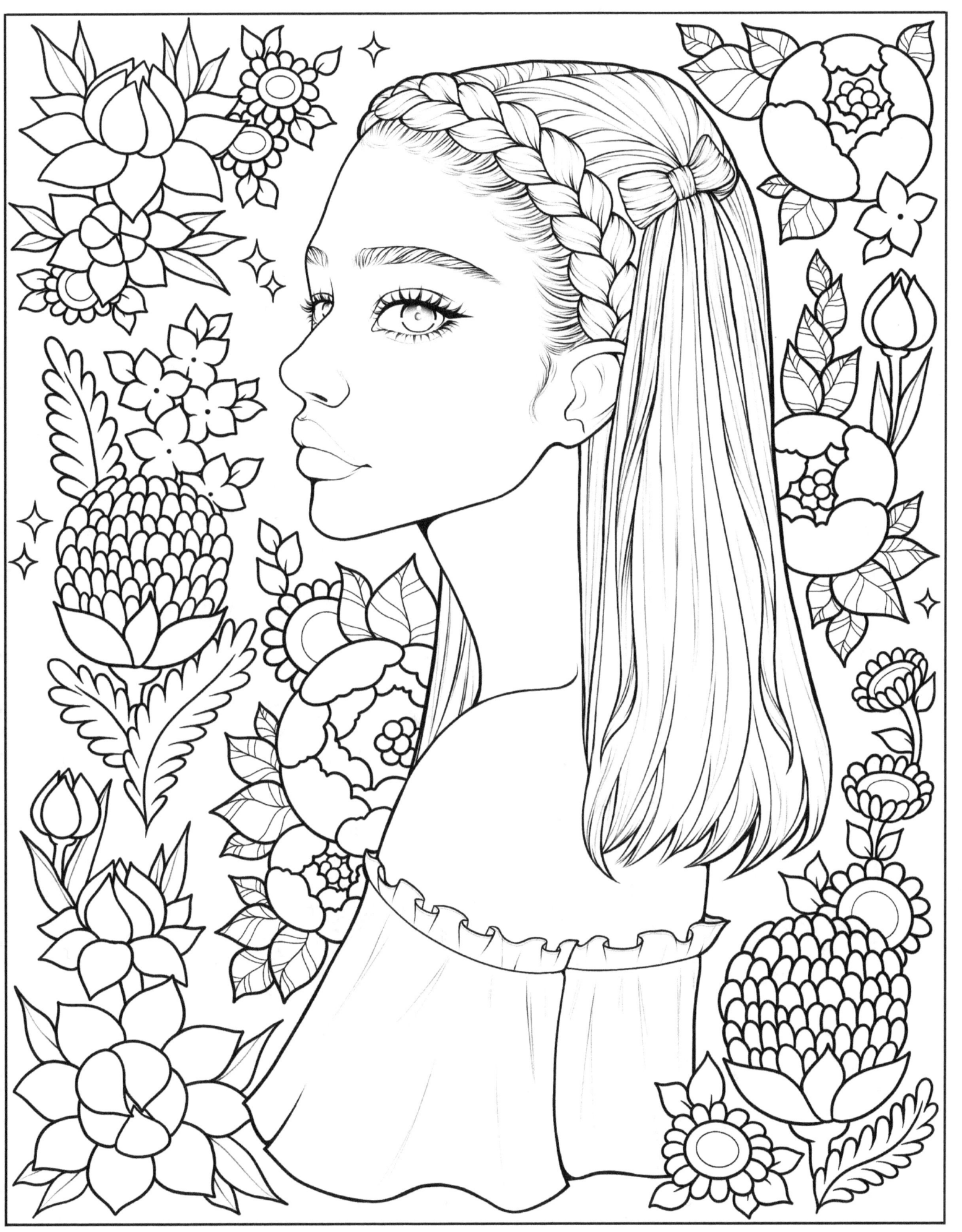

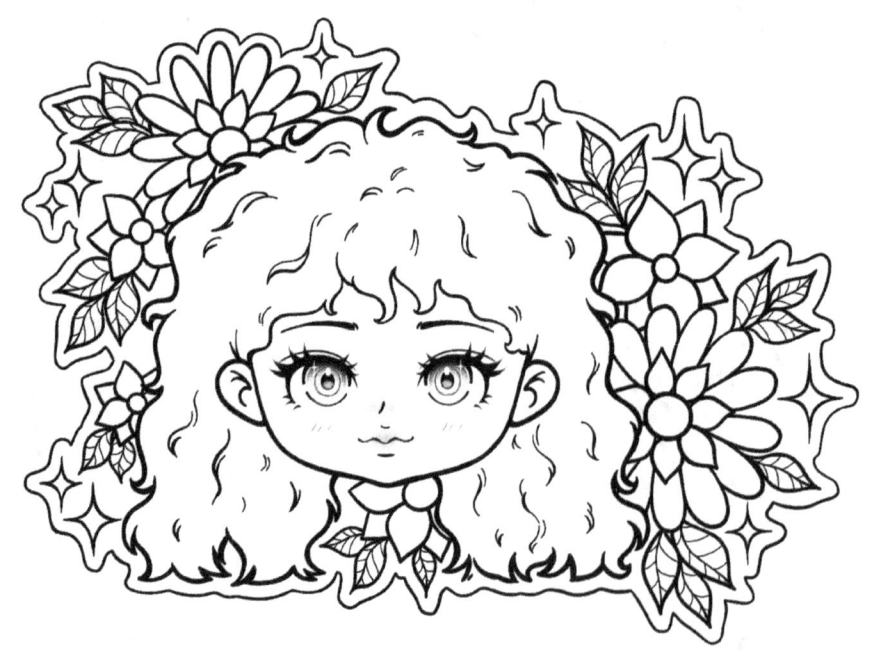

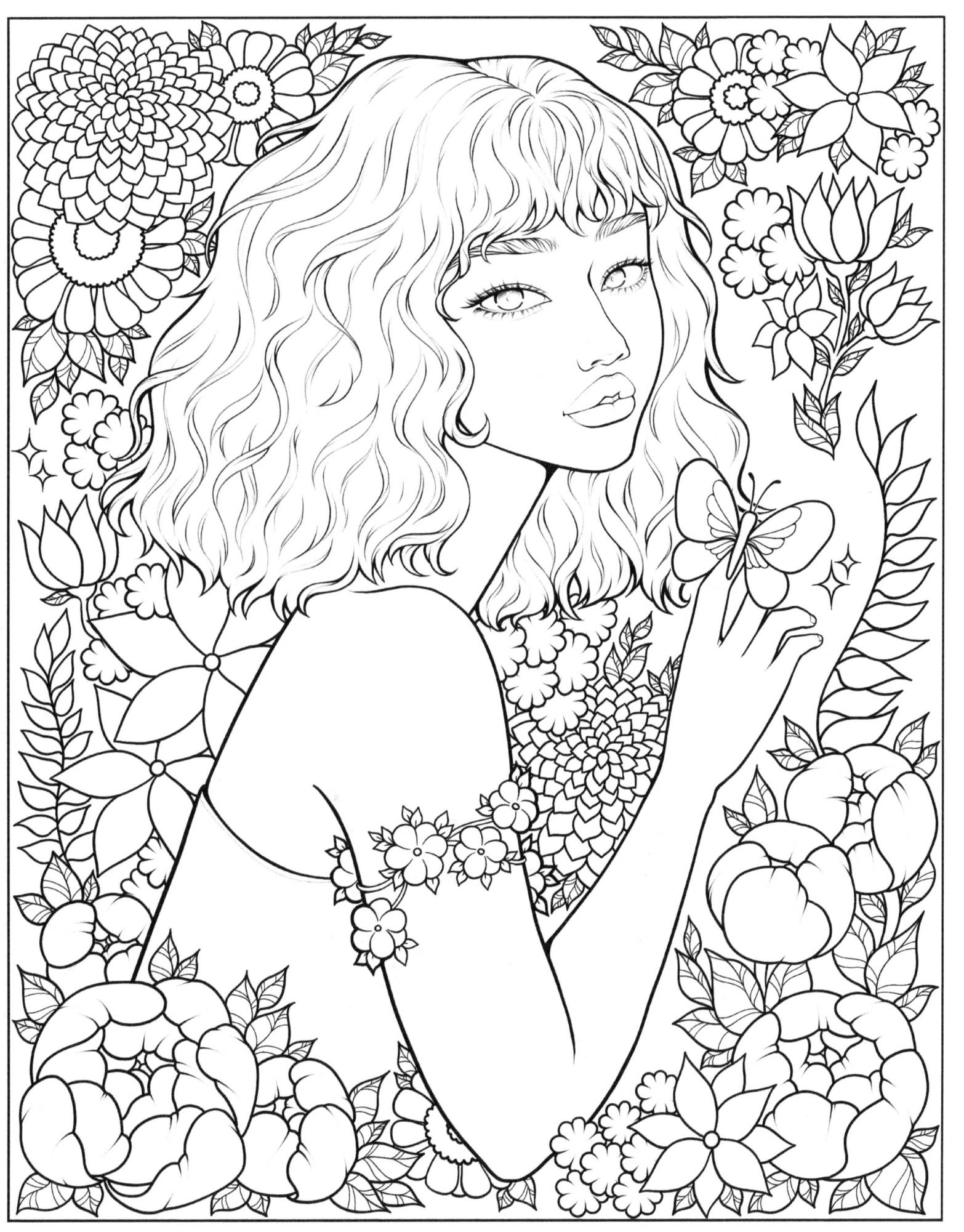

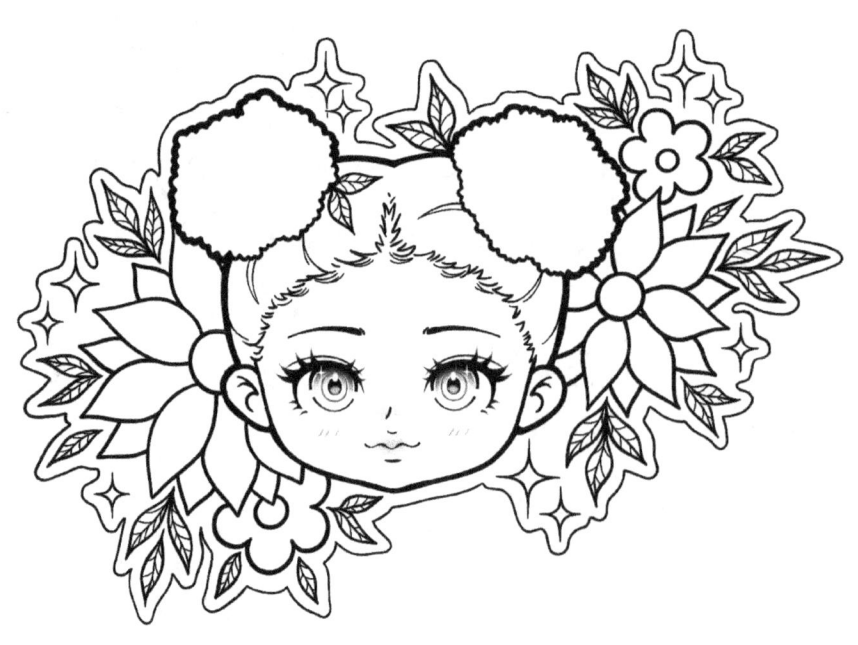

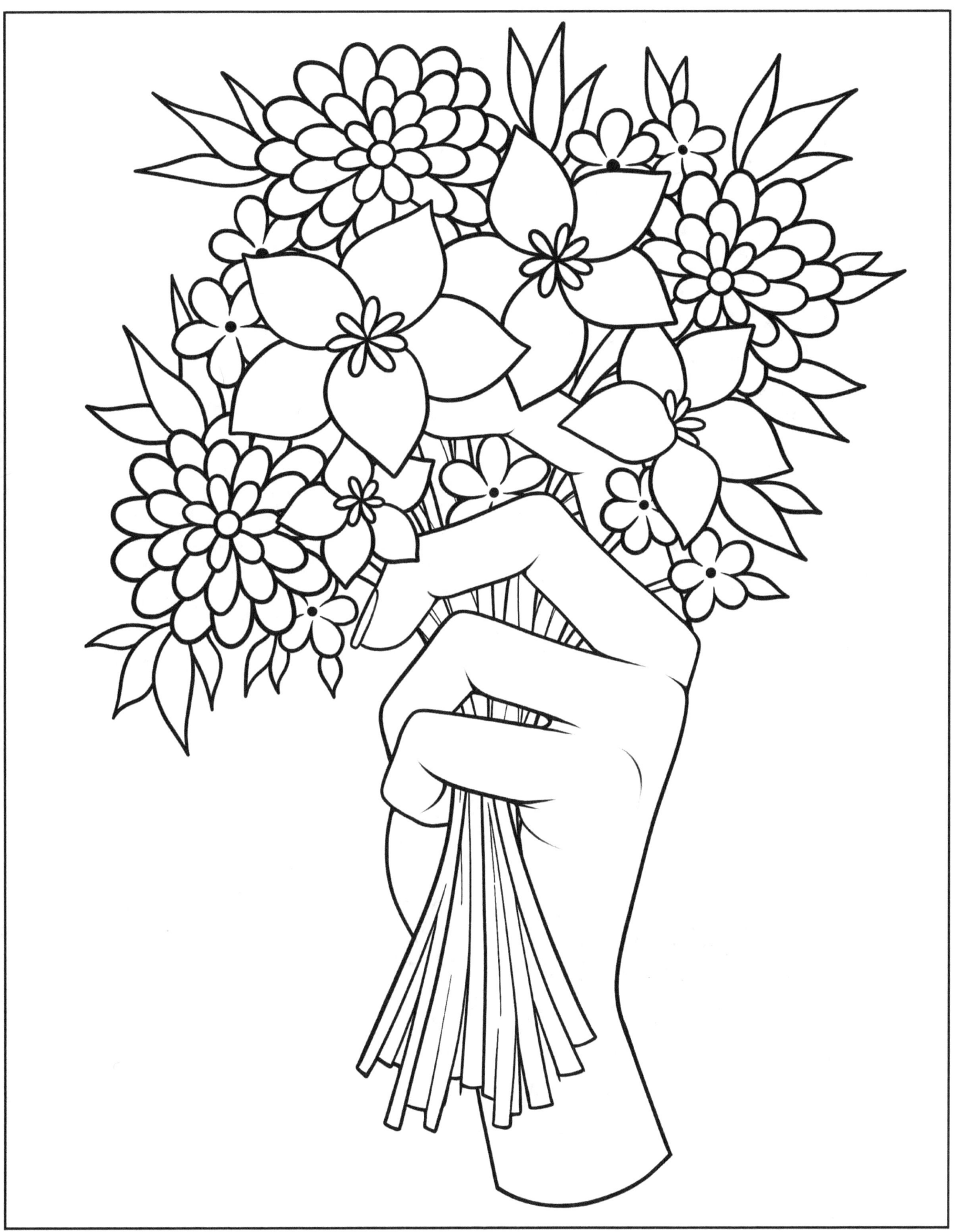

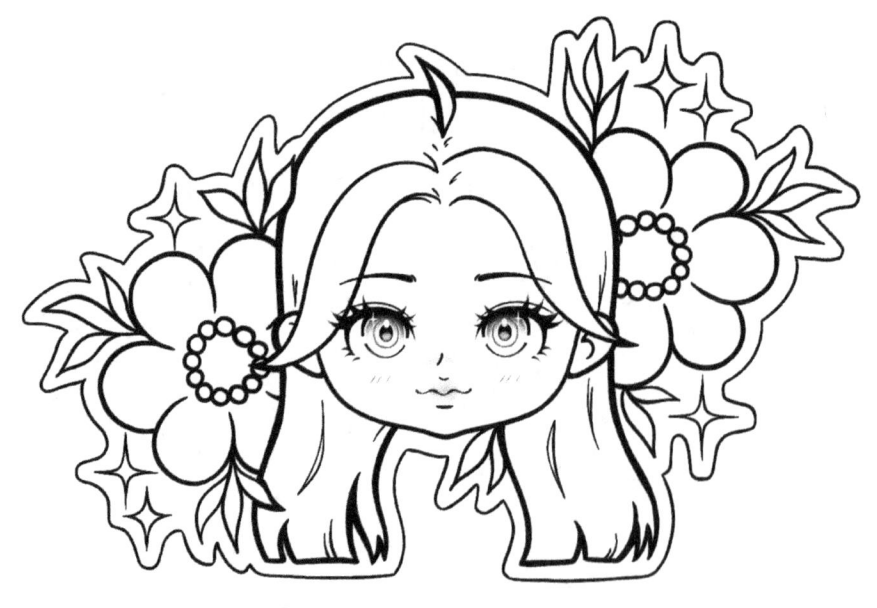

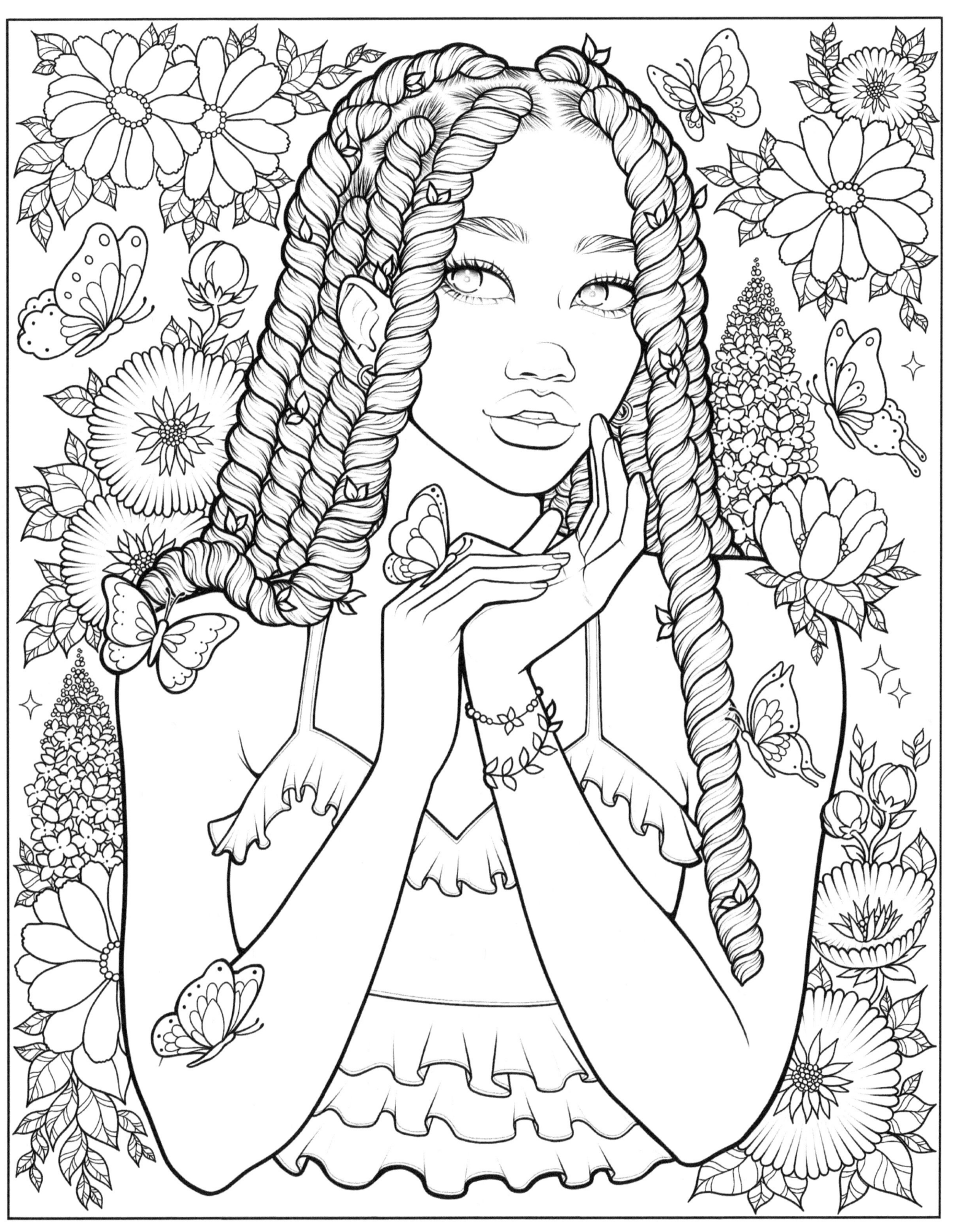

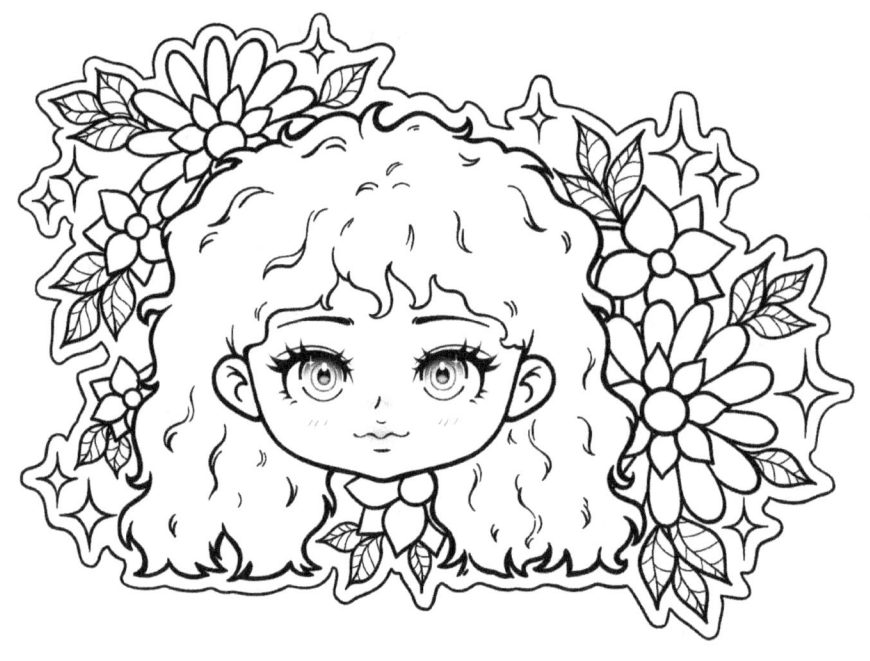

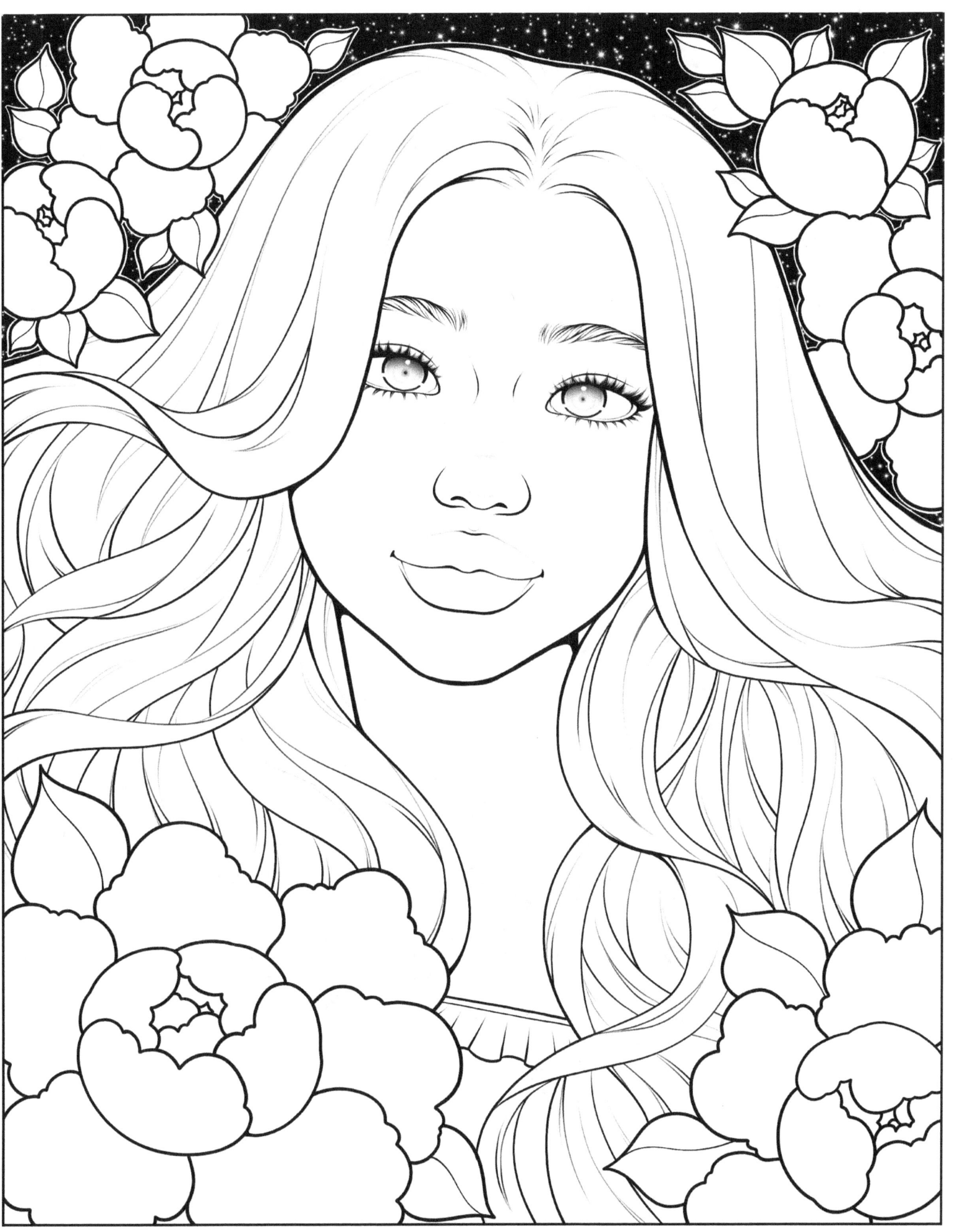

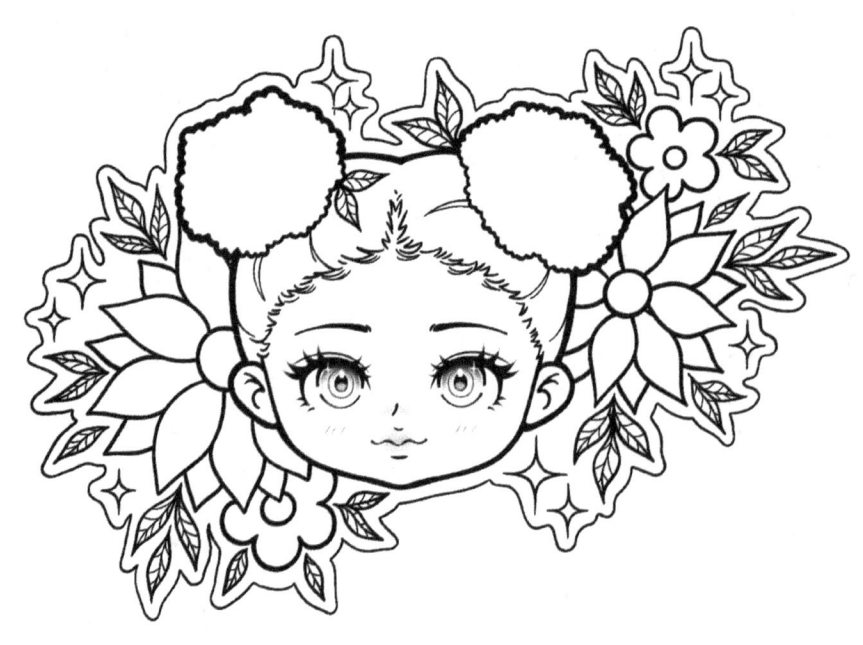

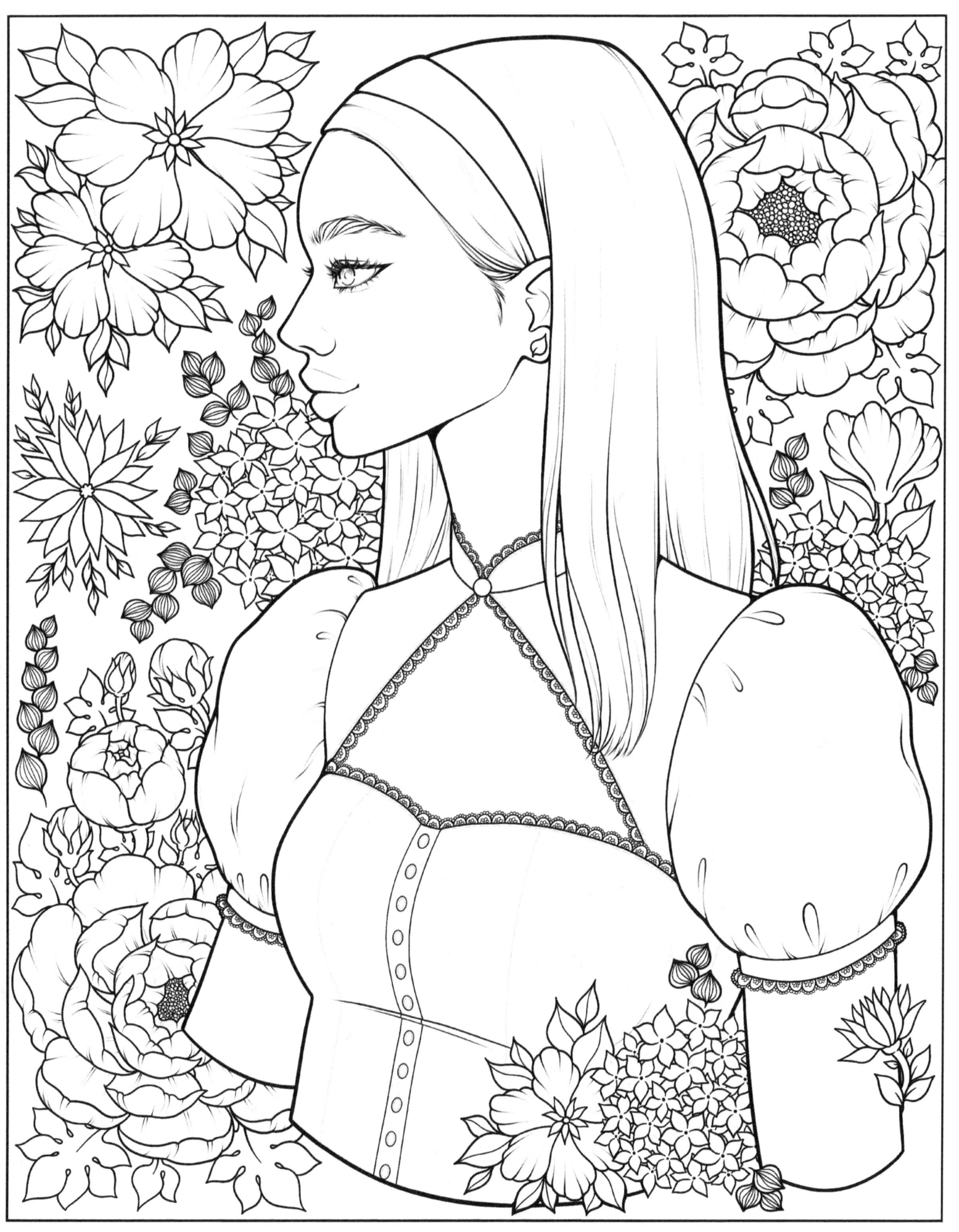

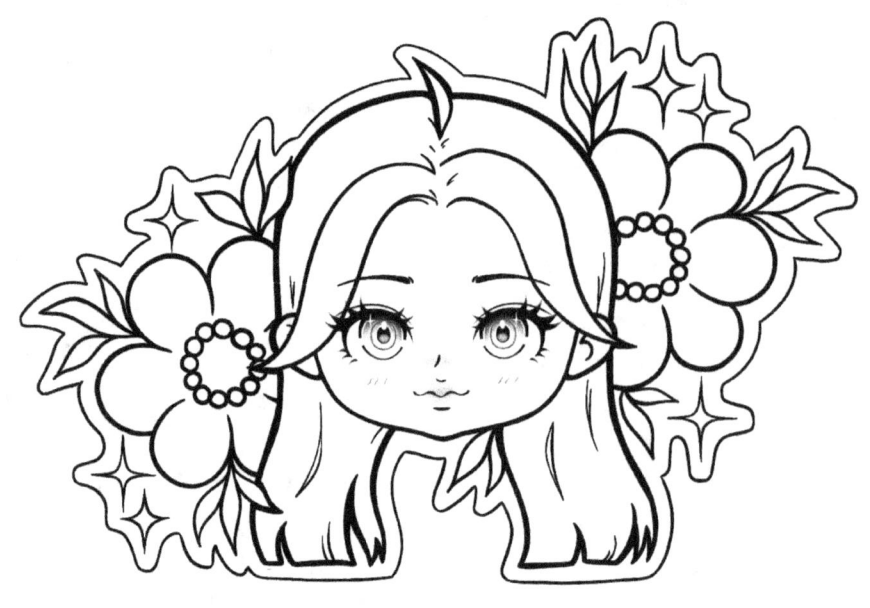

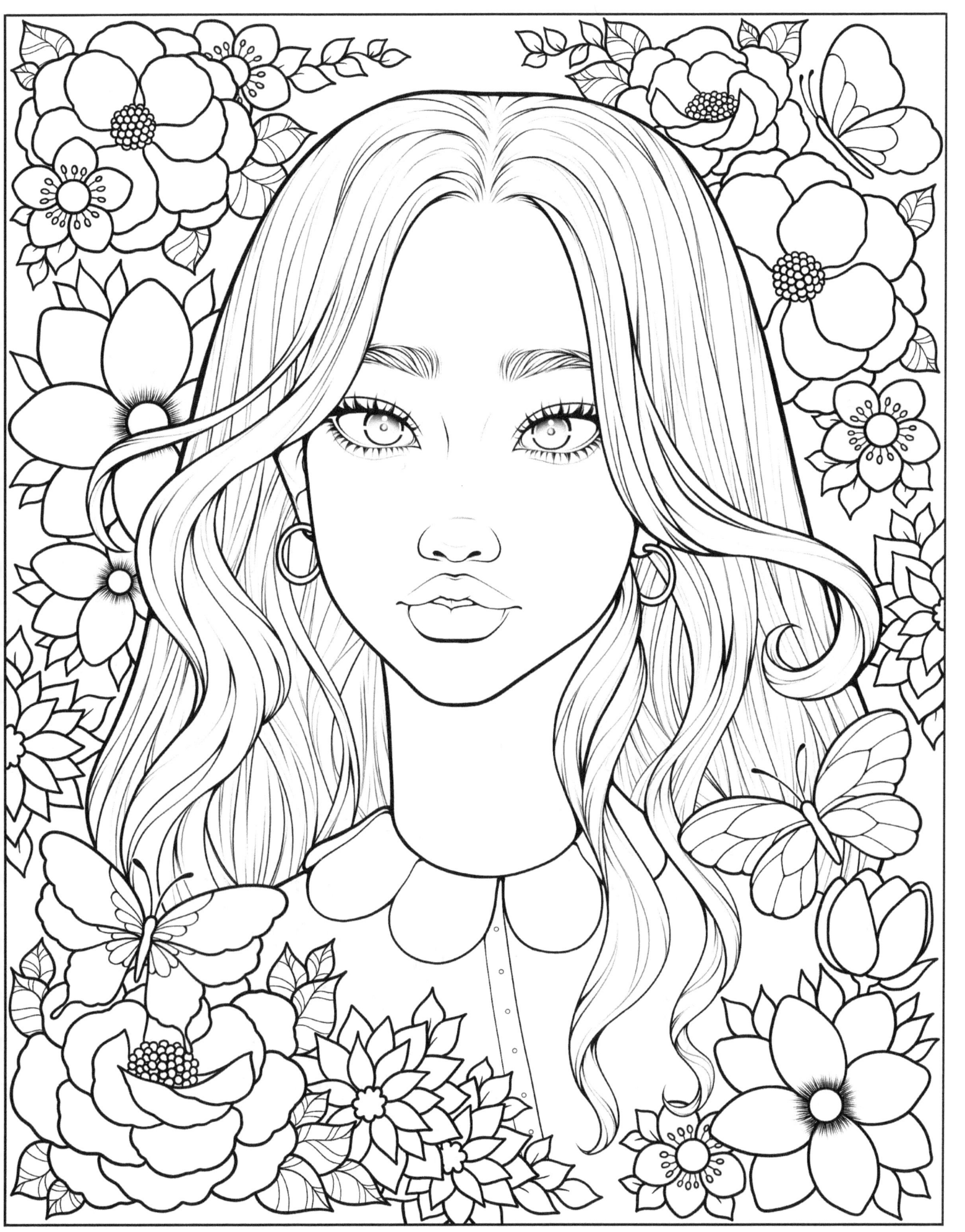

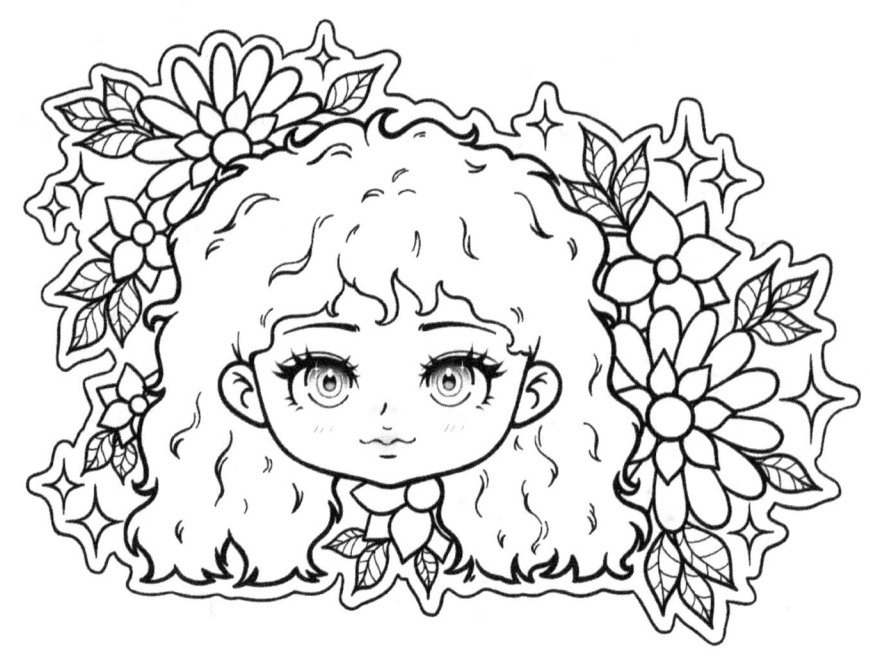

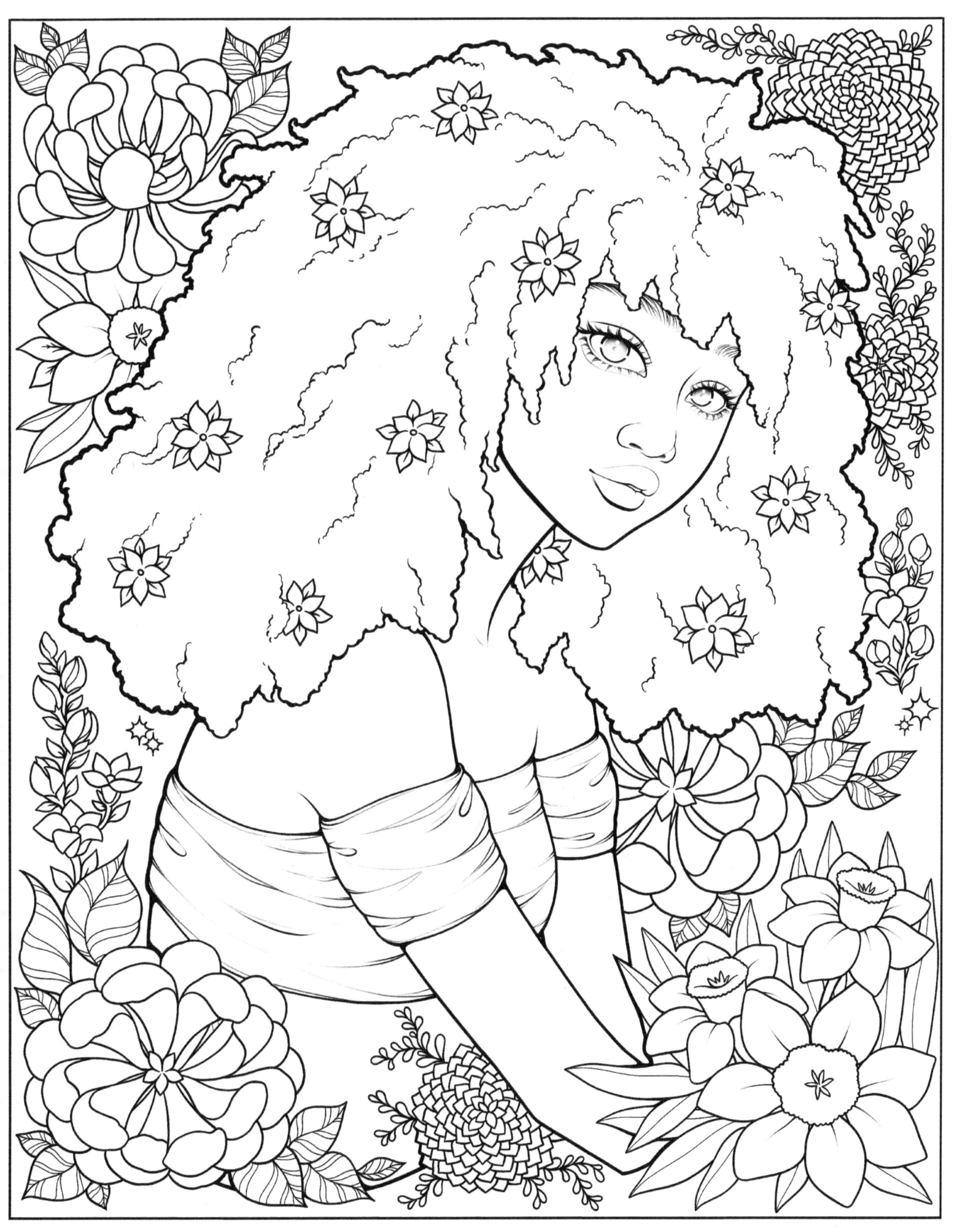

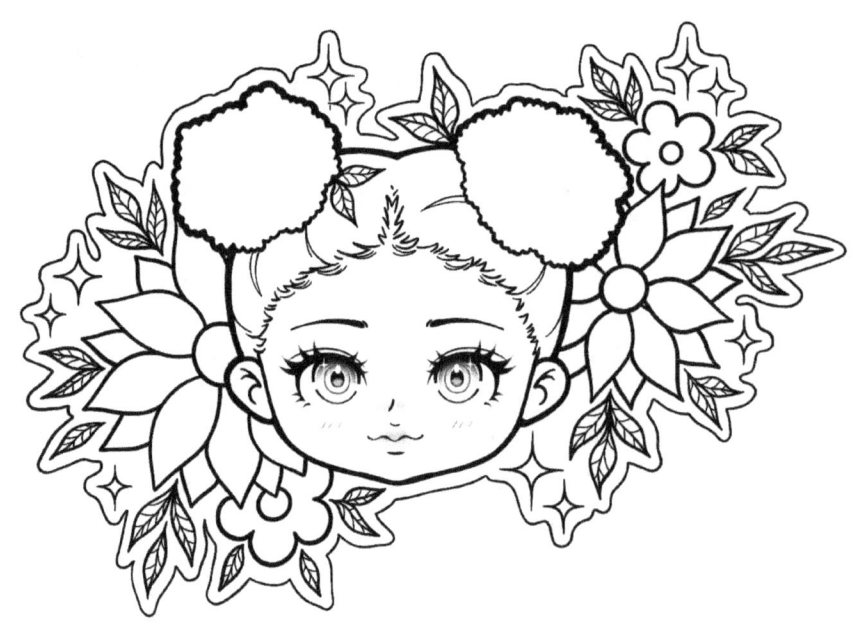

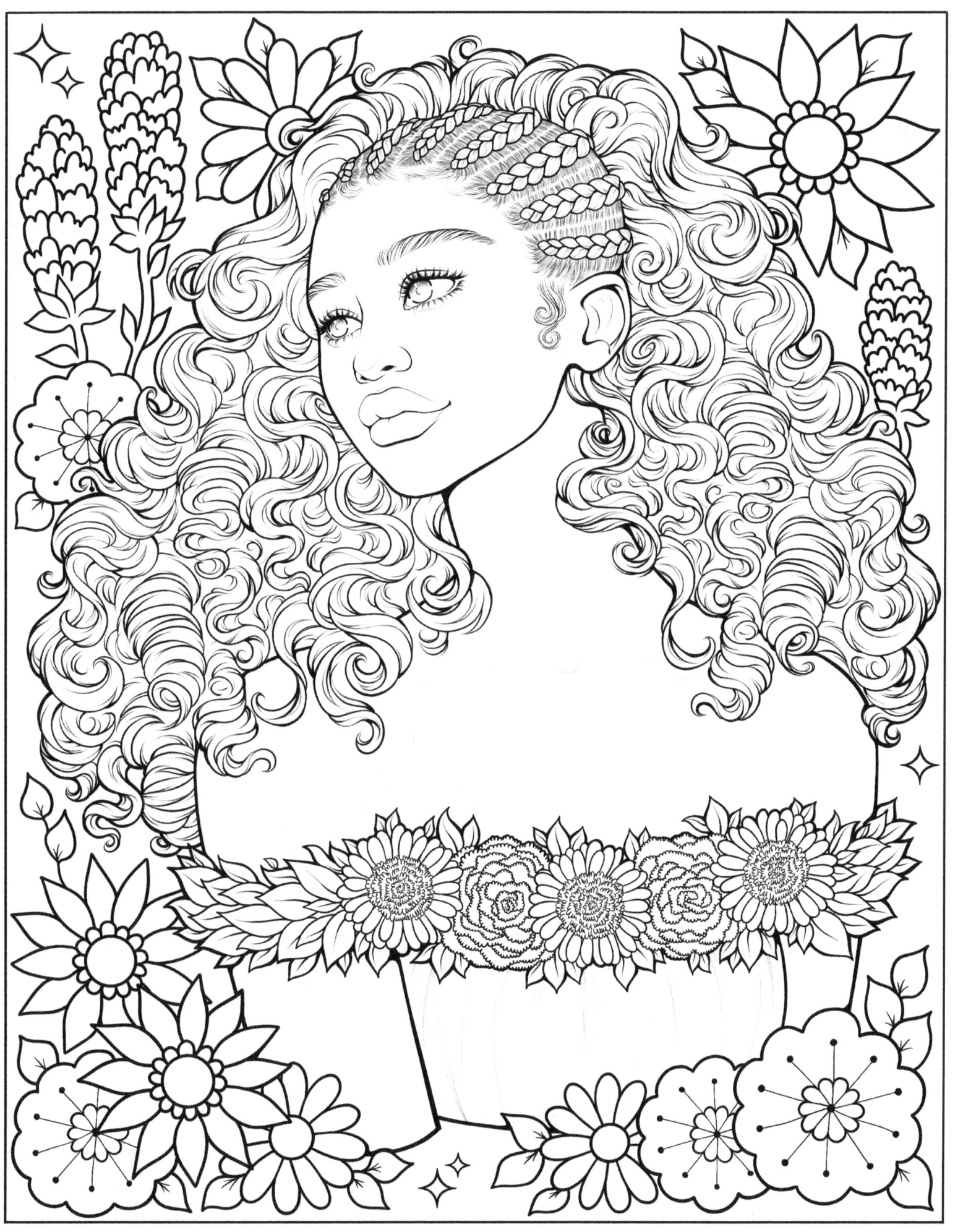

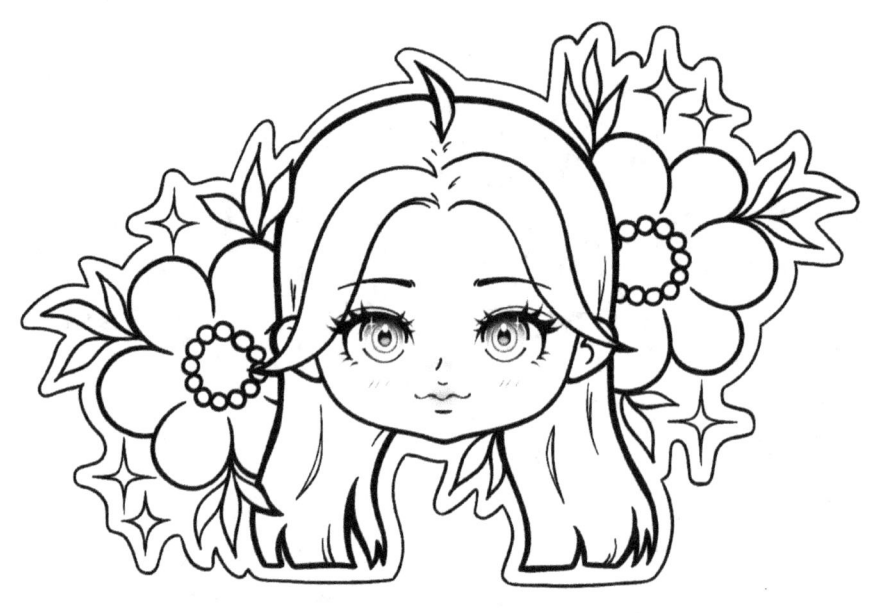

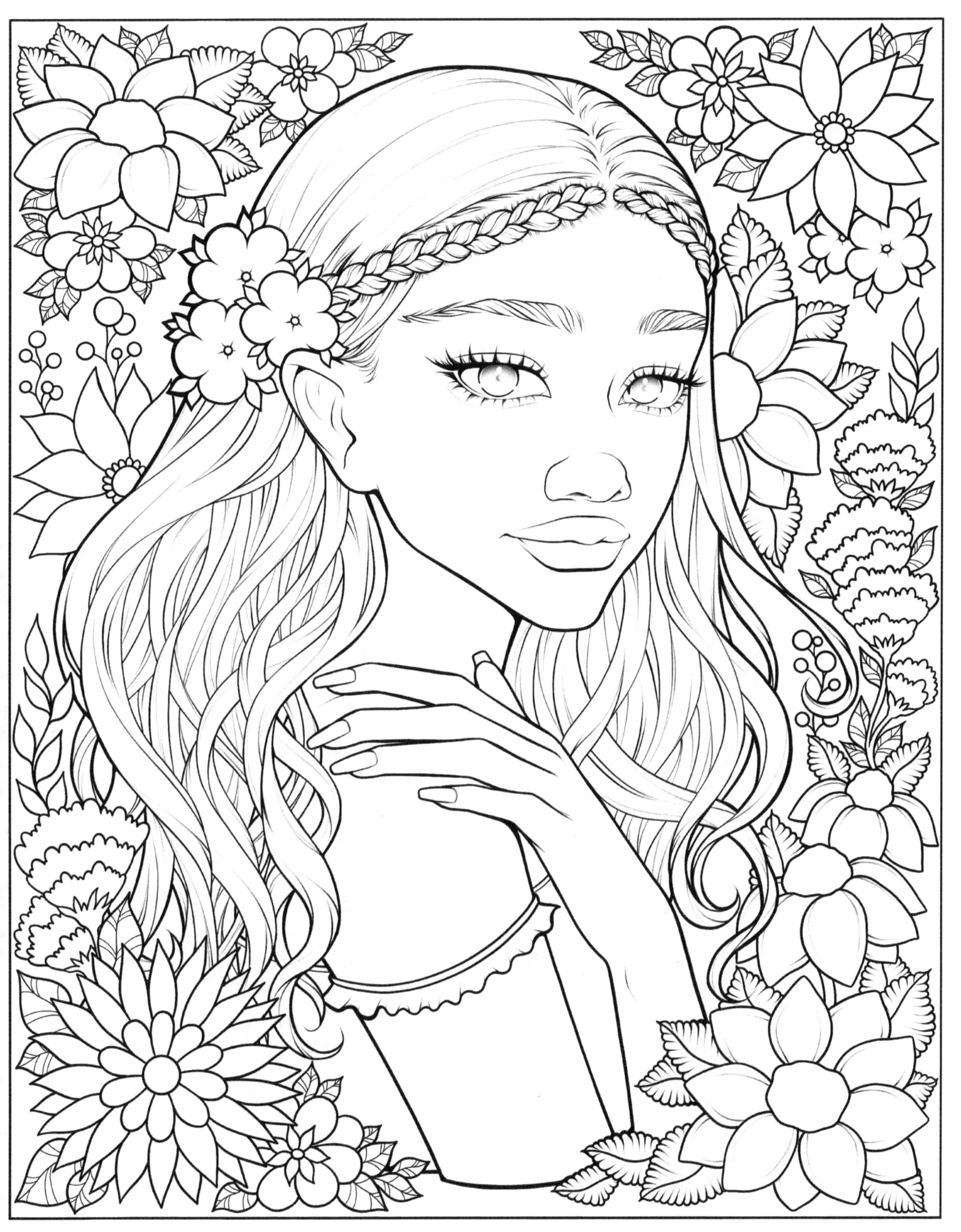

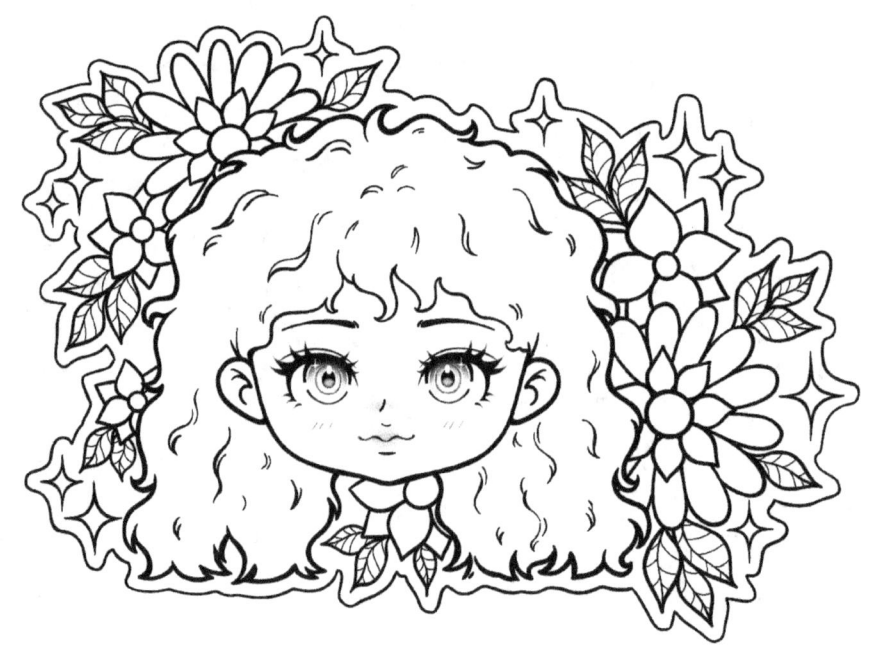

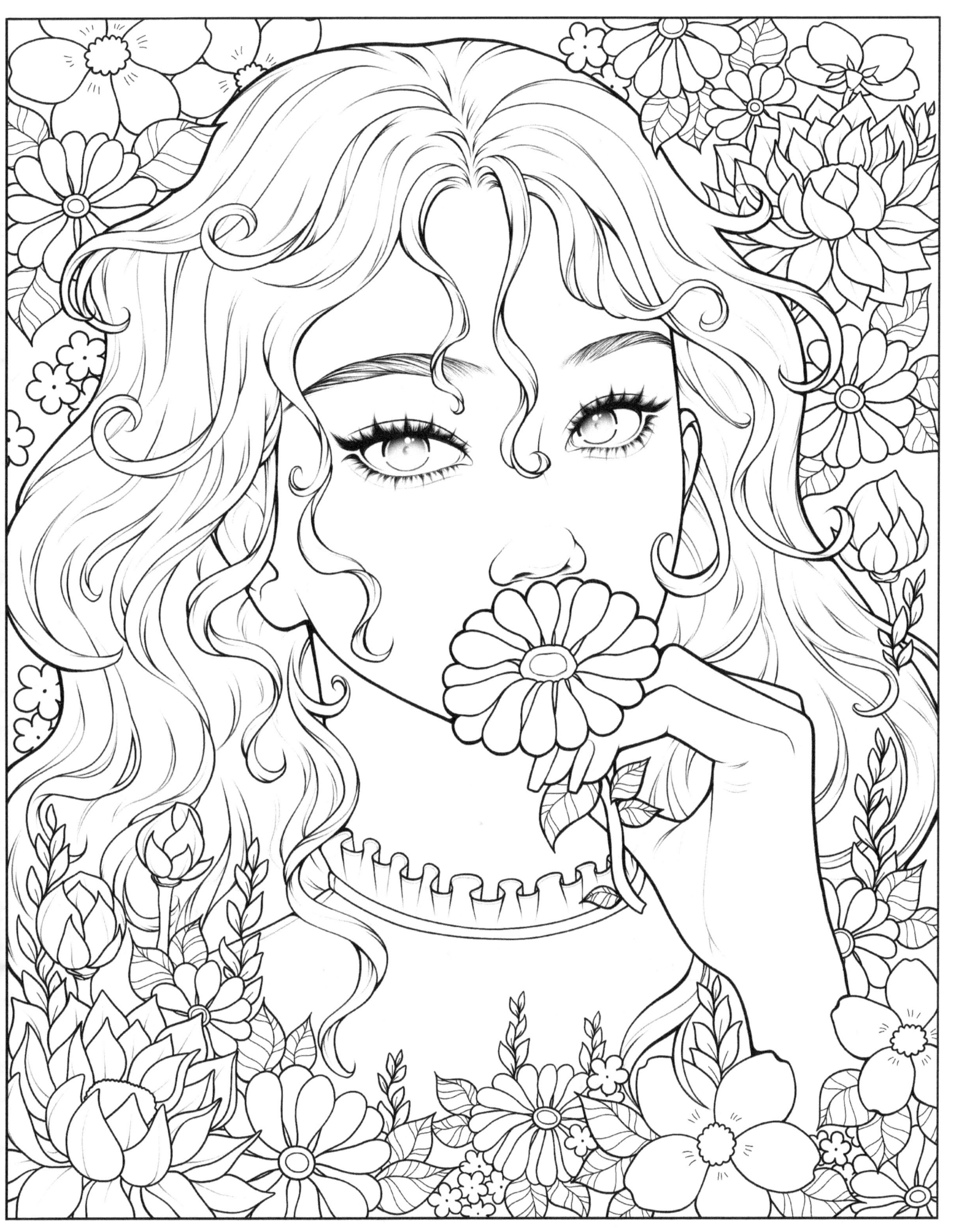

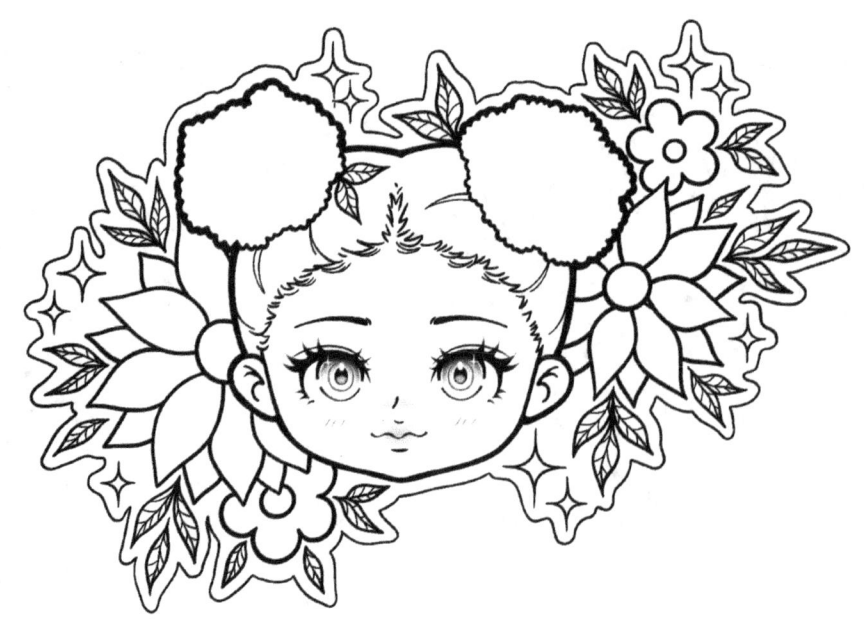

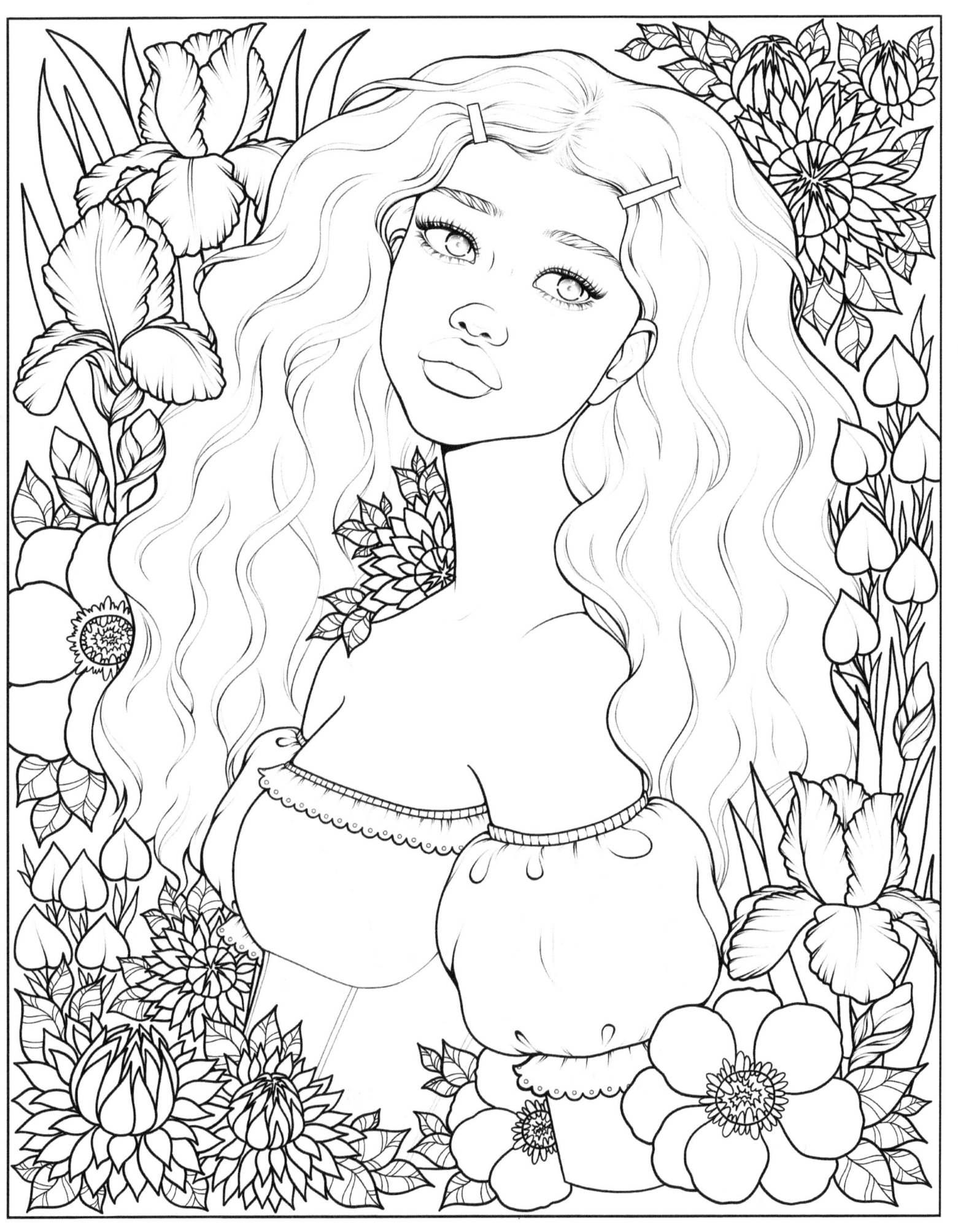

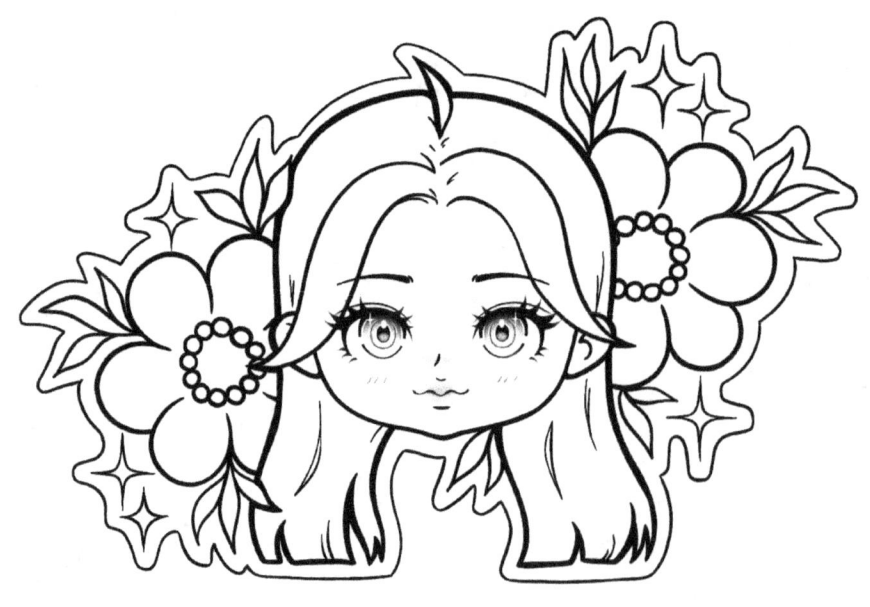

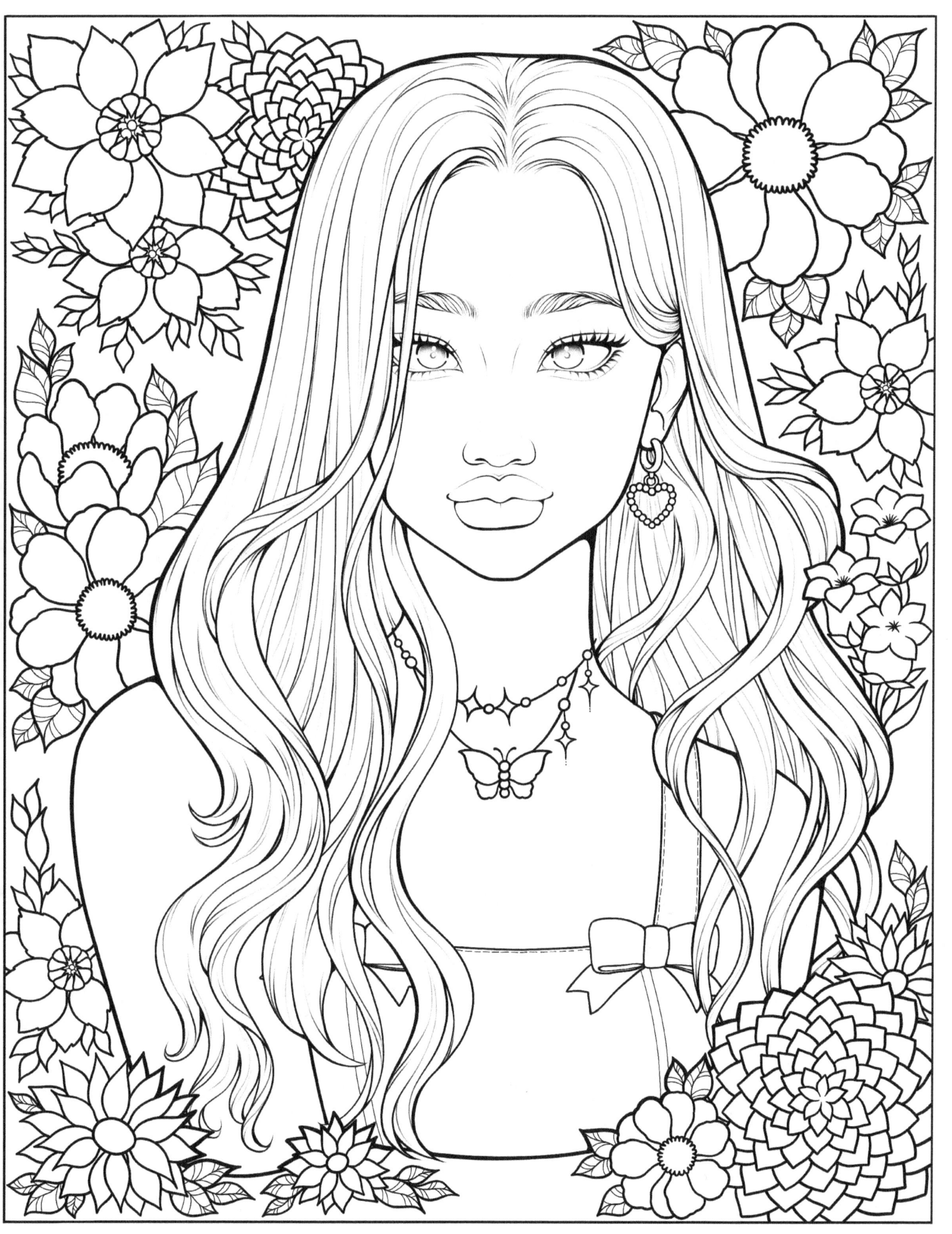

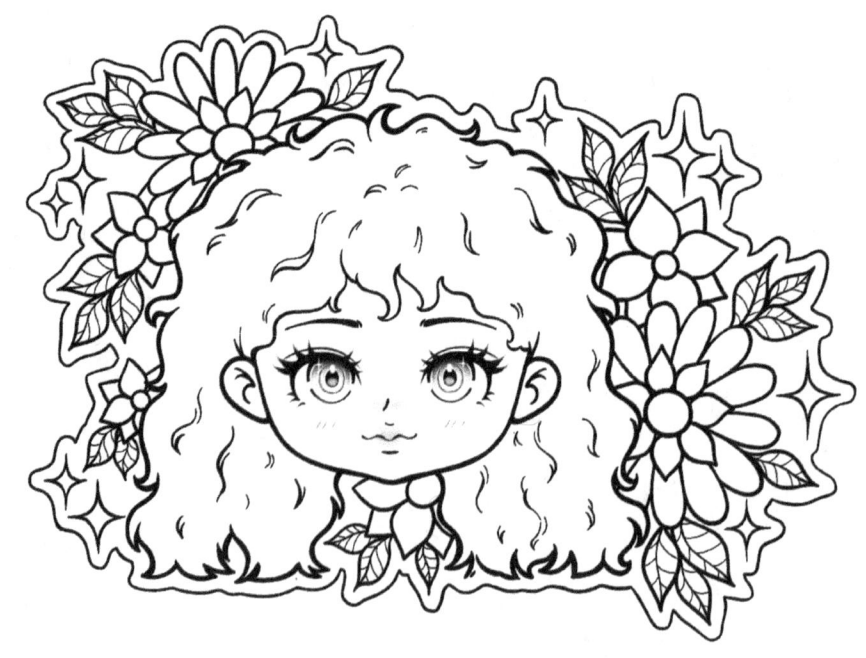

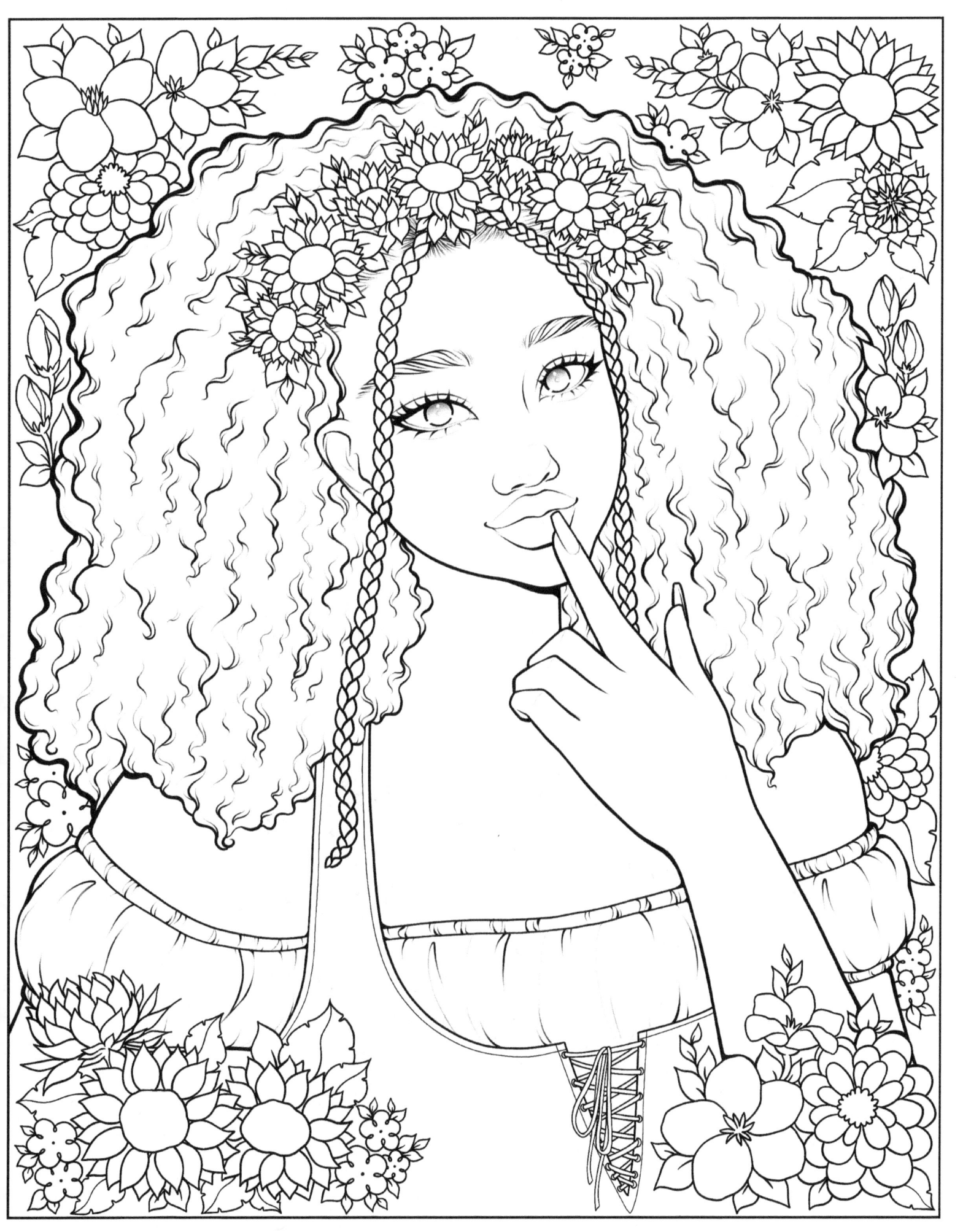

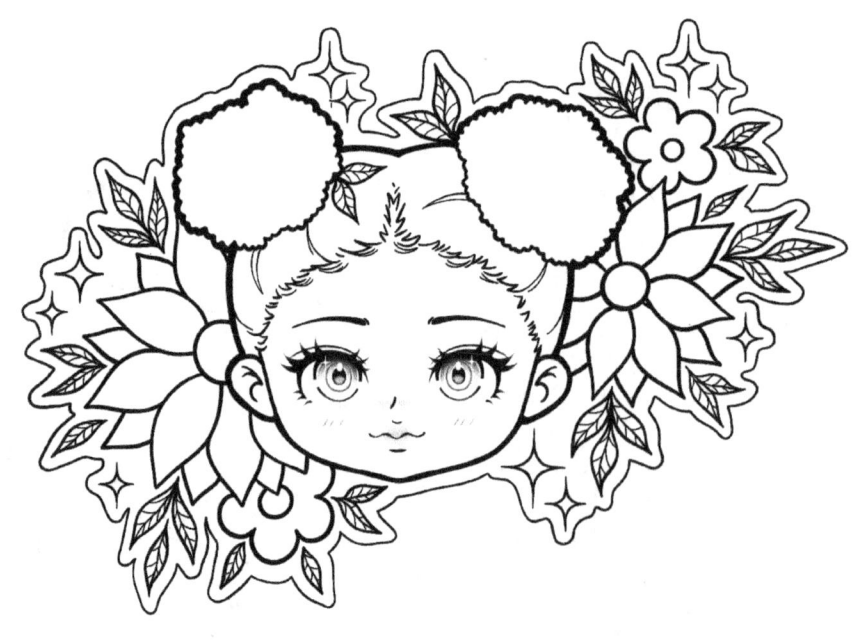

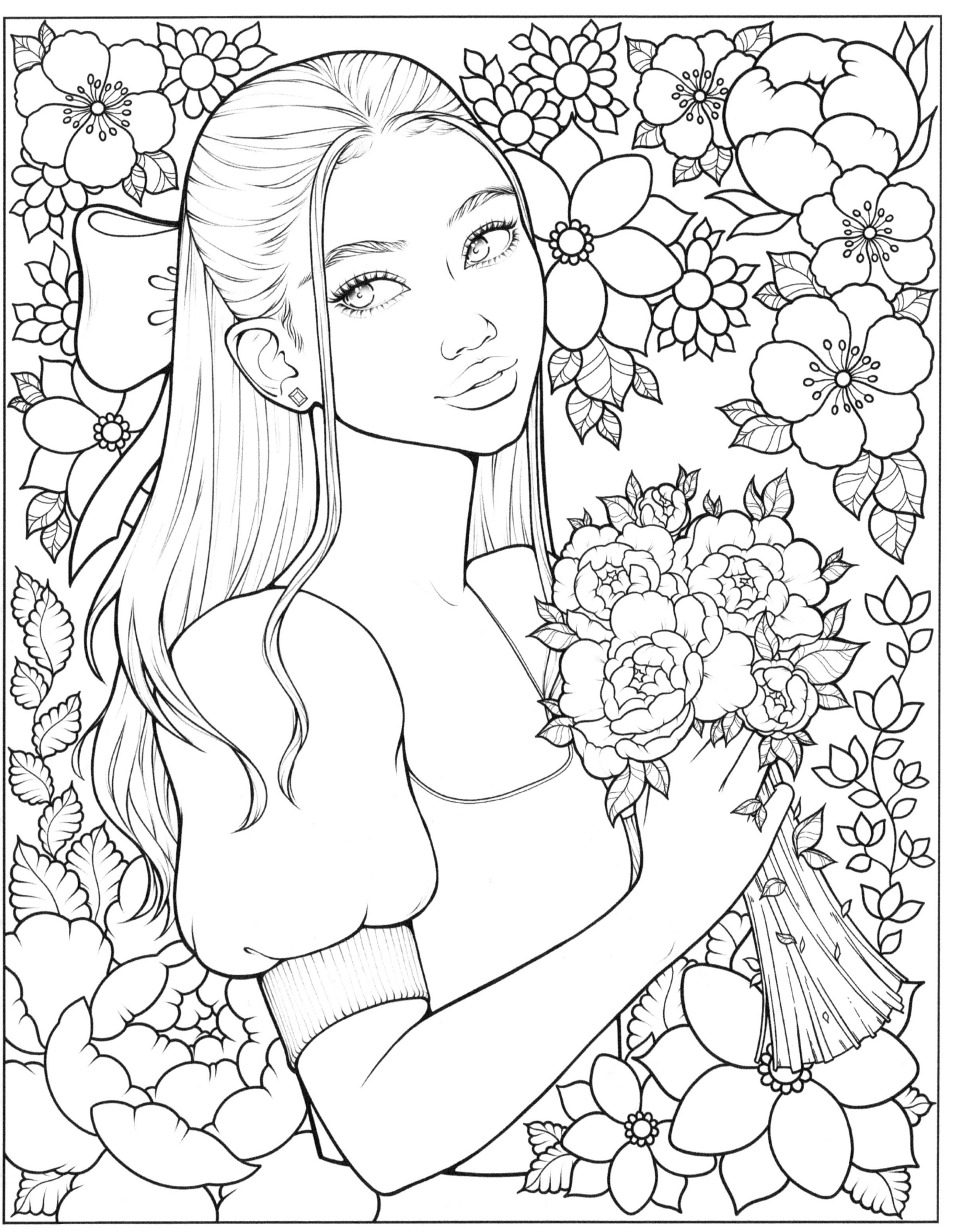

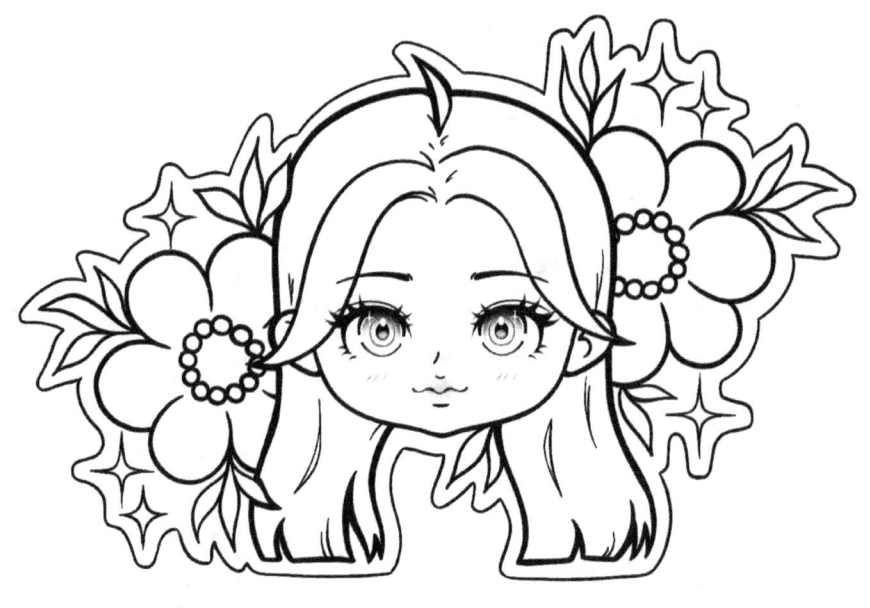

Bonus Page
"Flower Girls Vol.3" Coloring Book

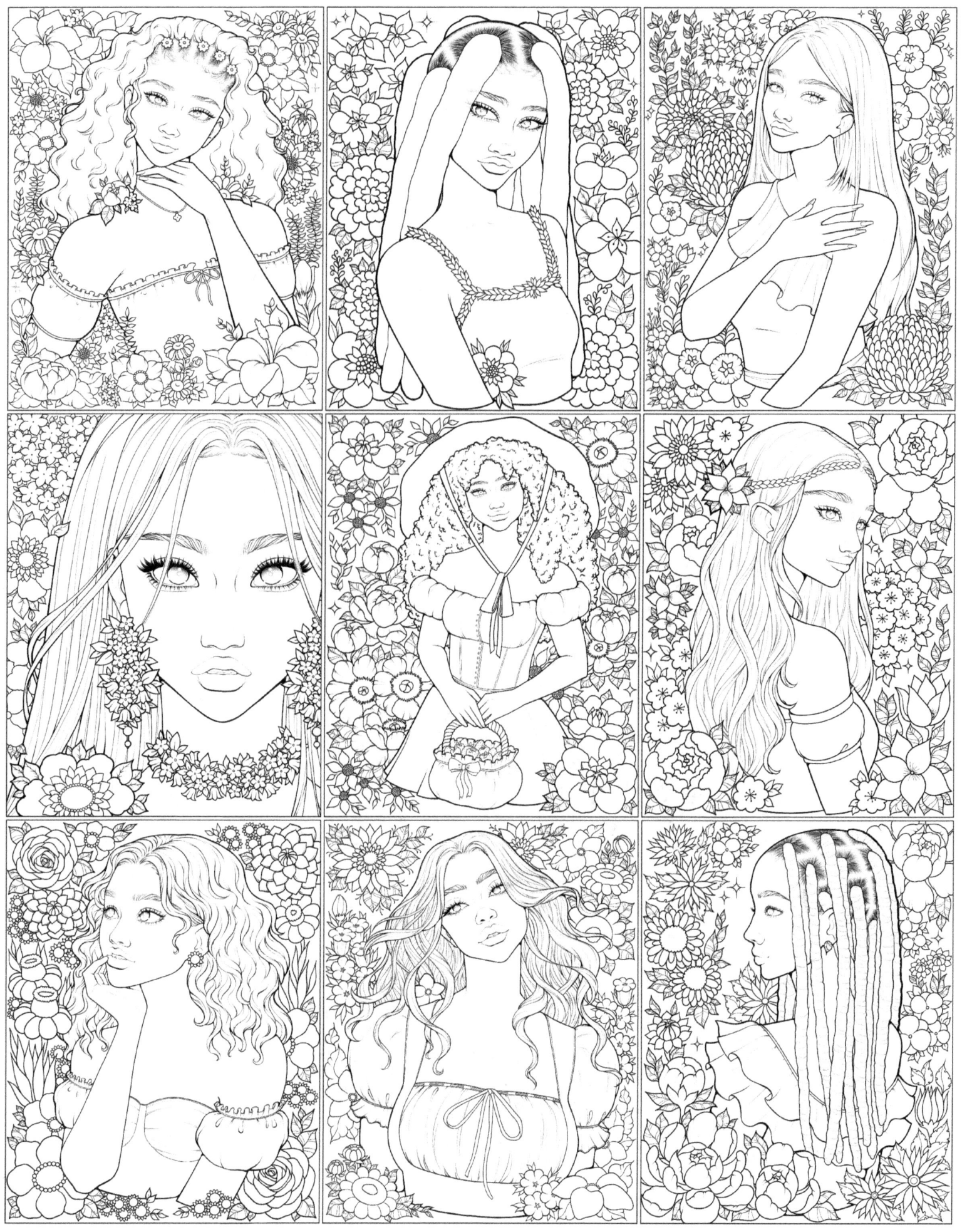

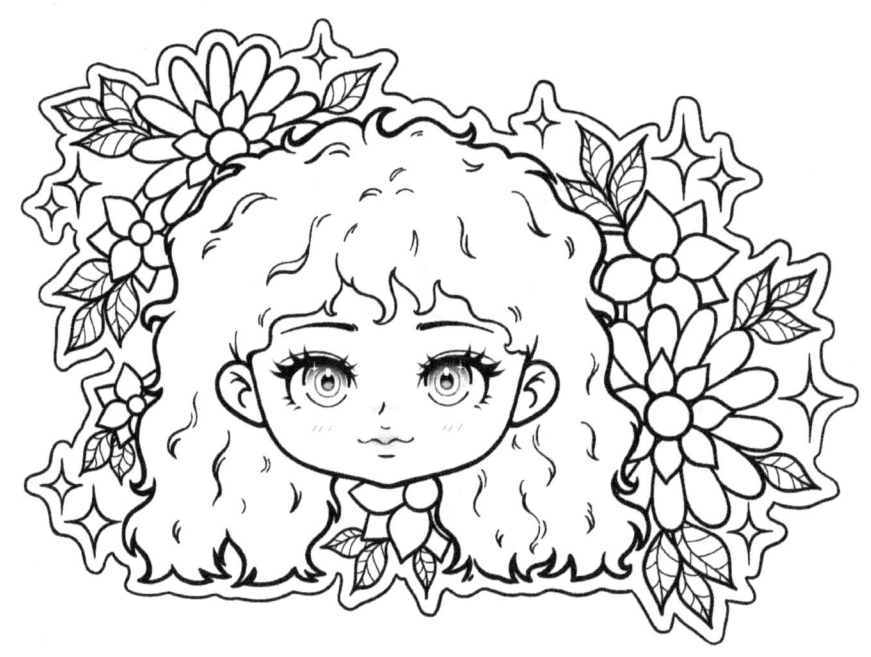

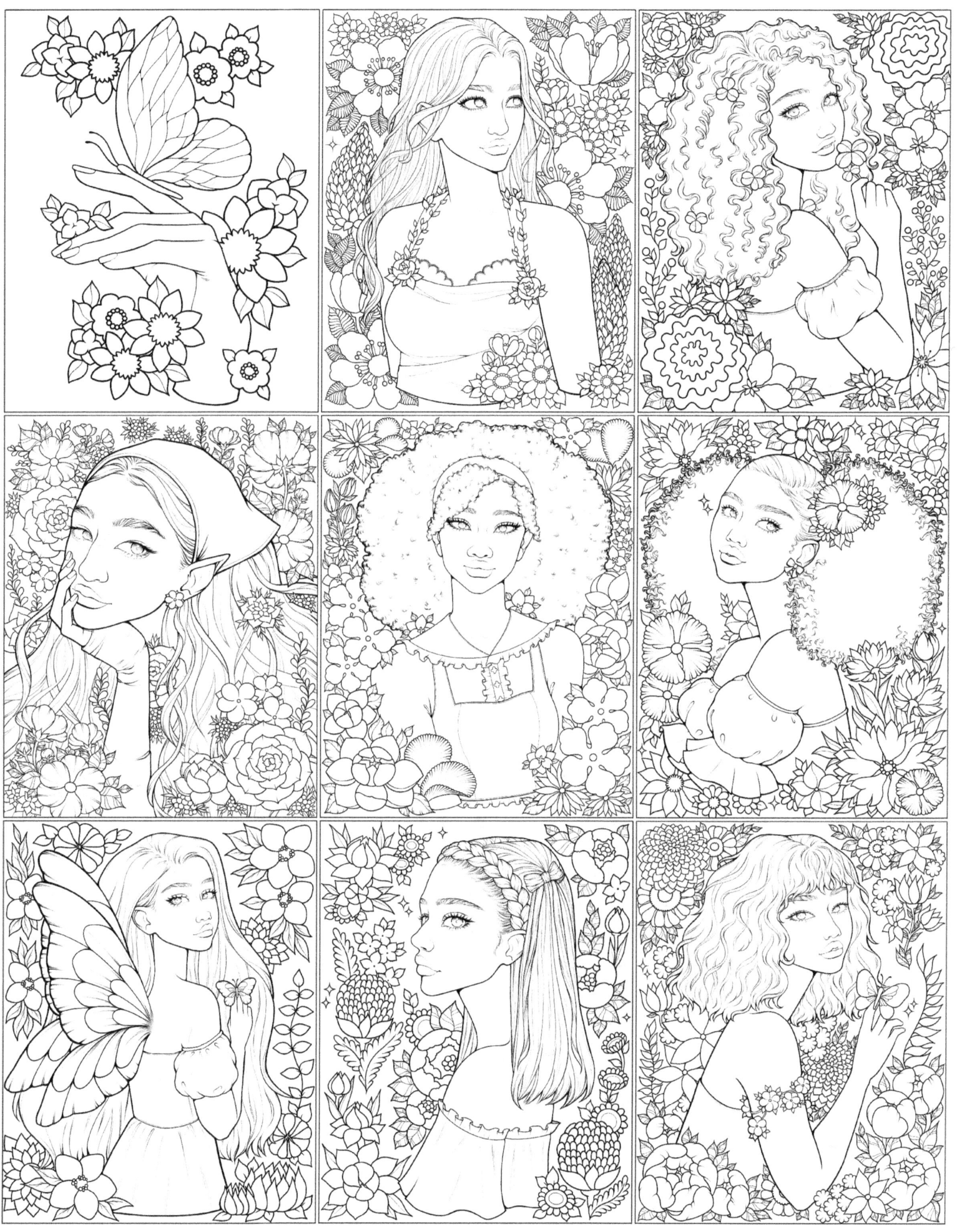

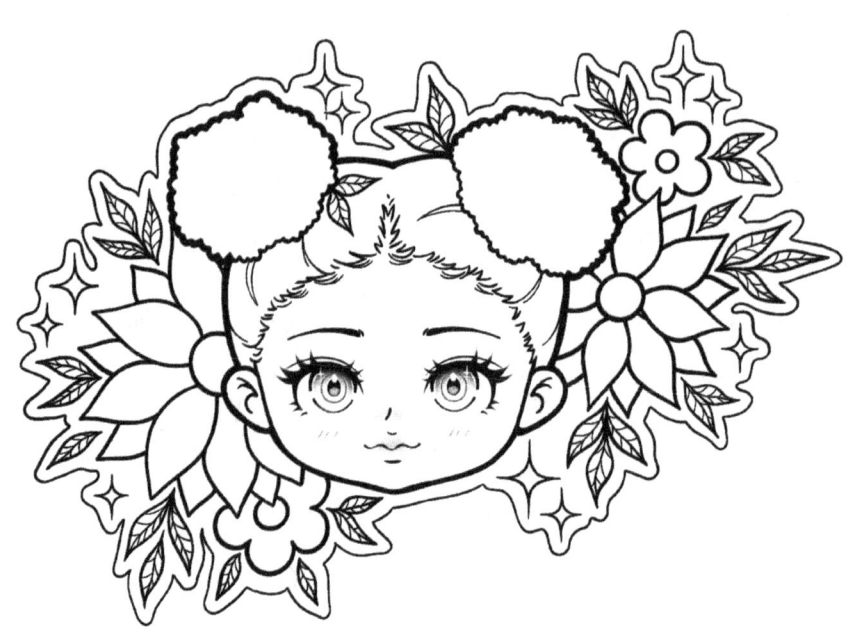

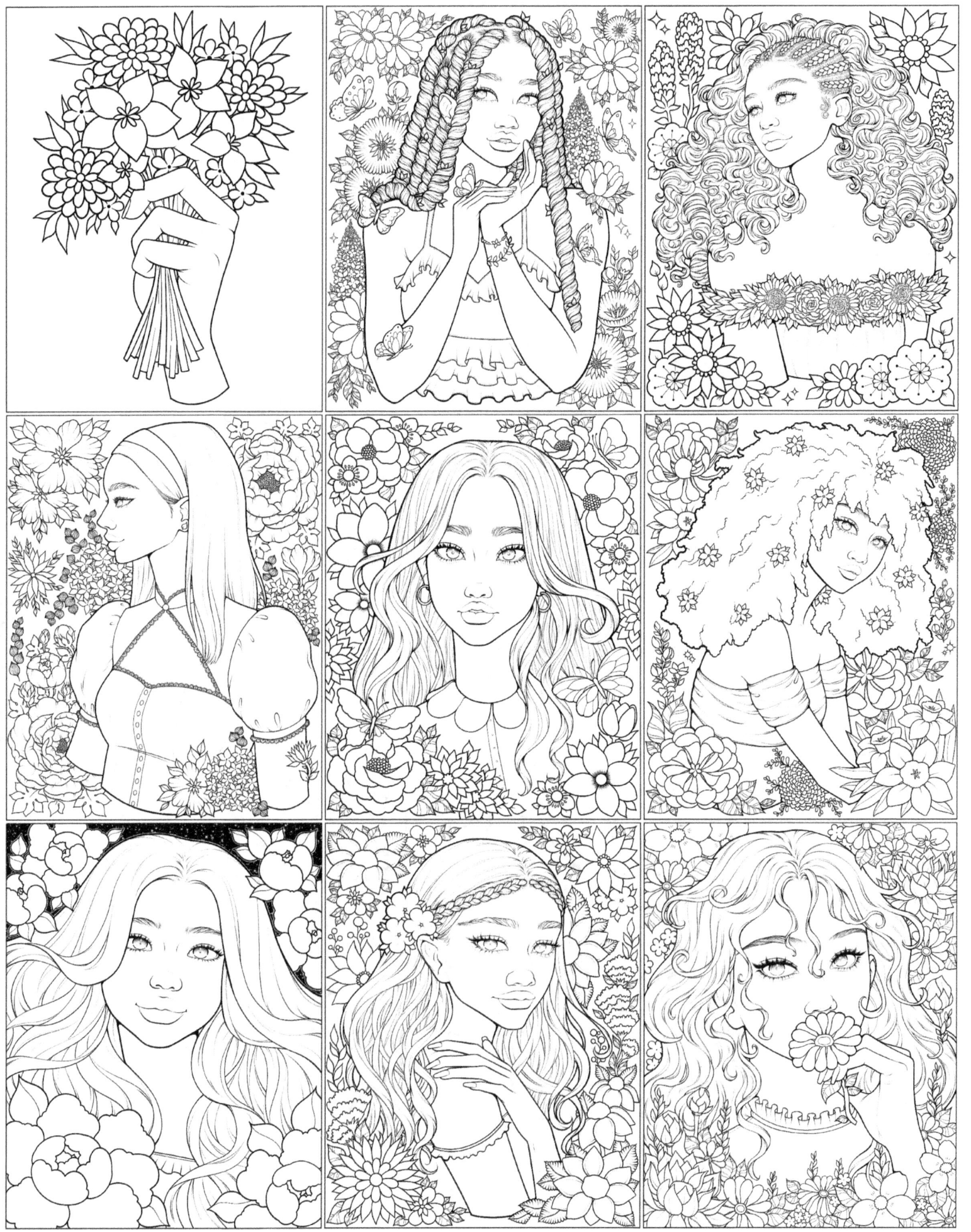

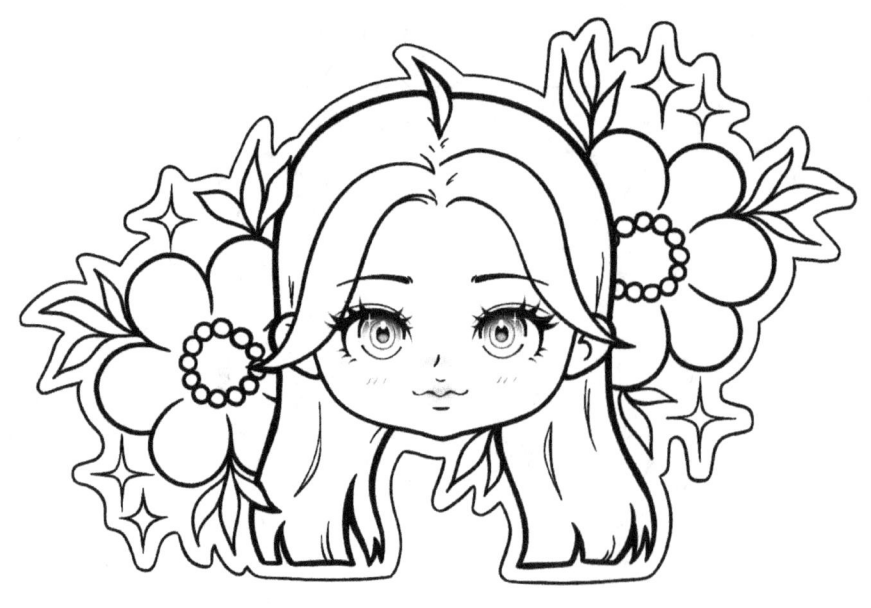

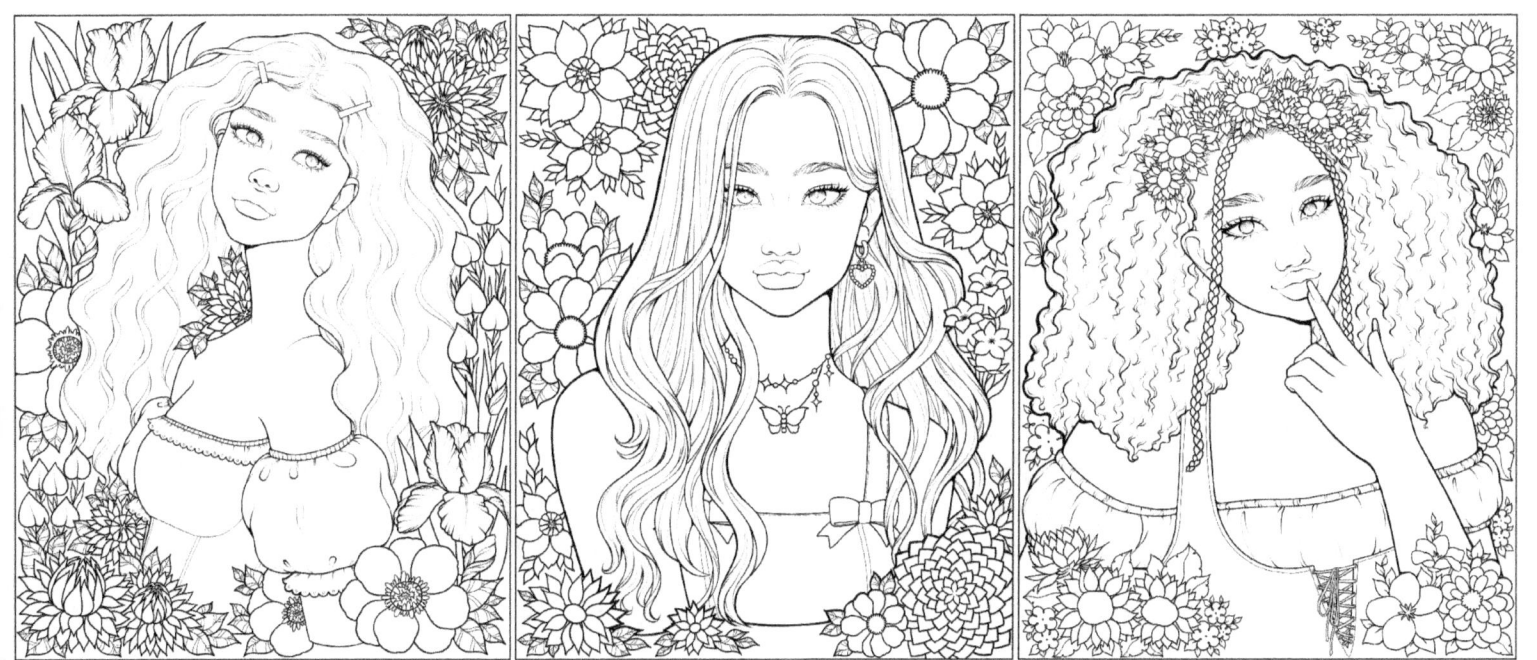

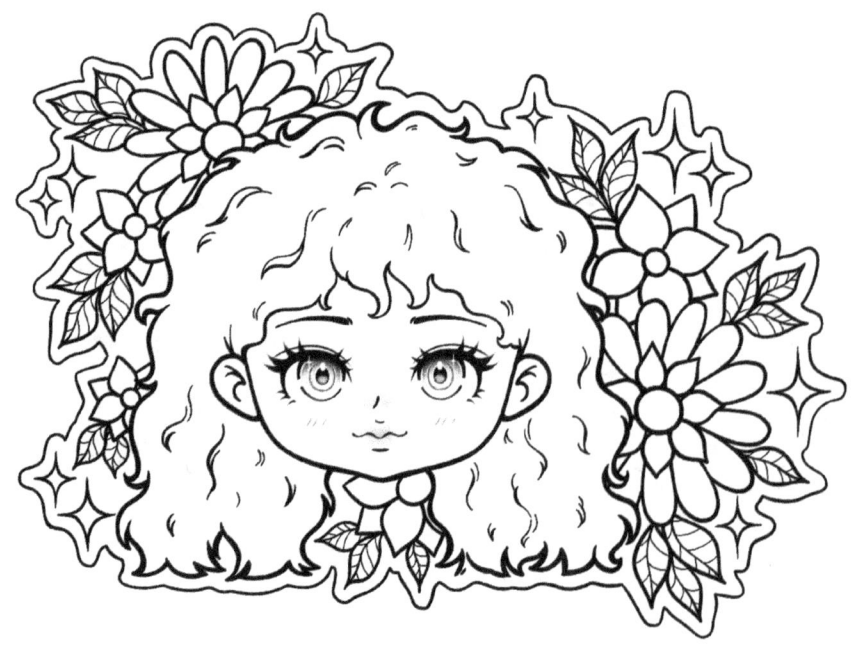

COLOR TEST PAGE

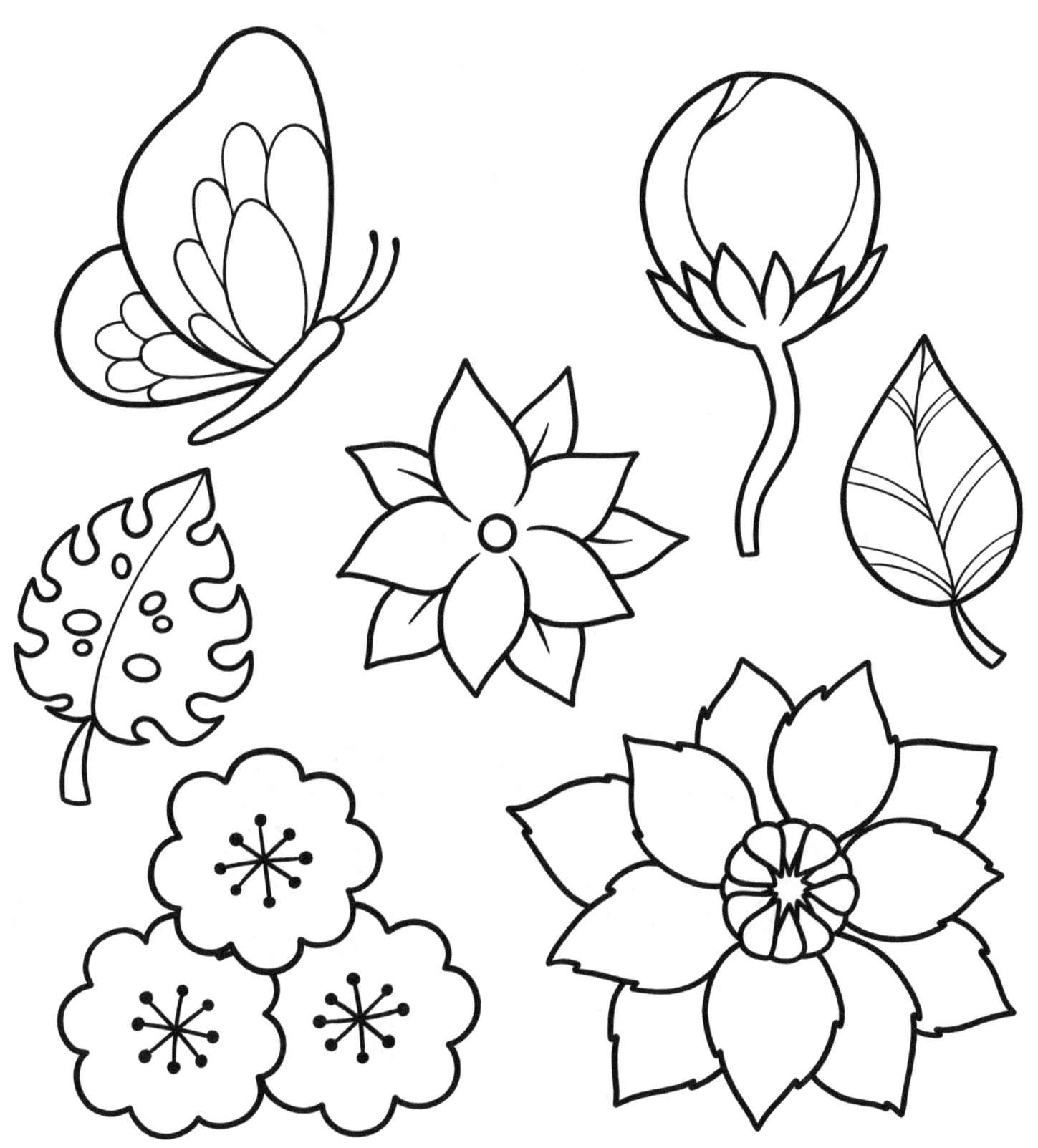

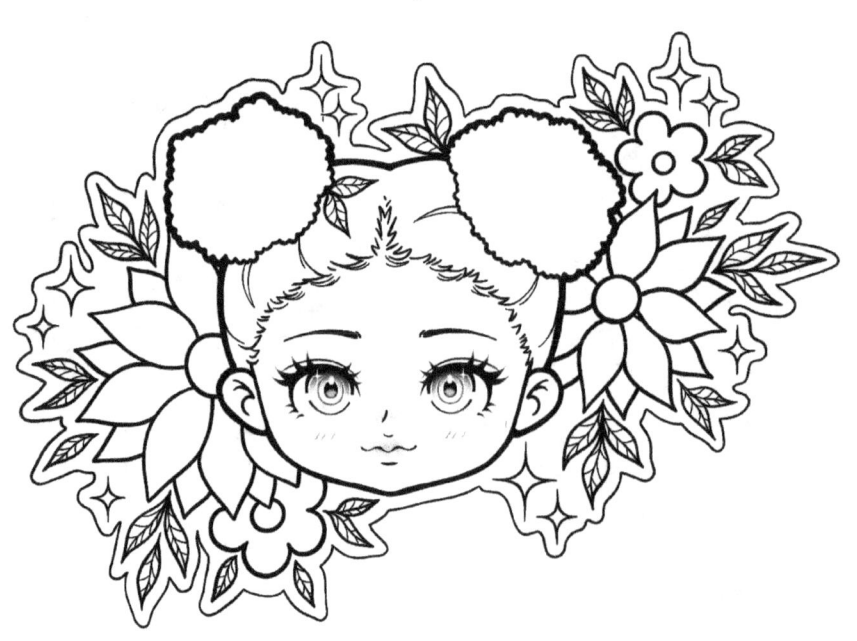

More books by emzdrawings:

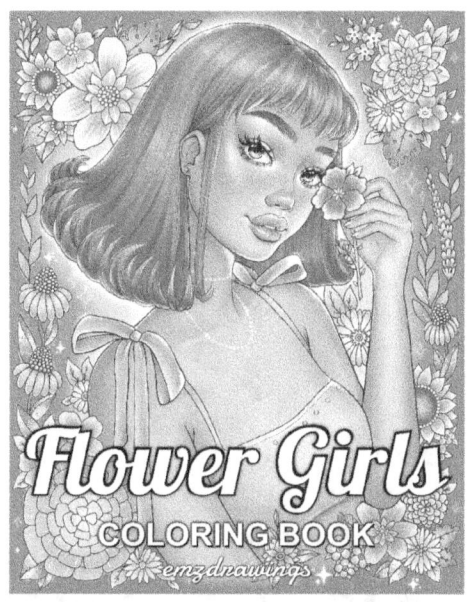

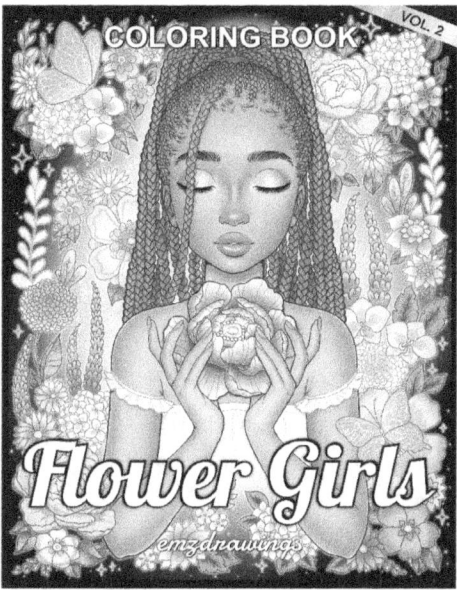

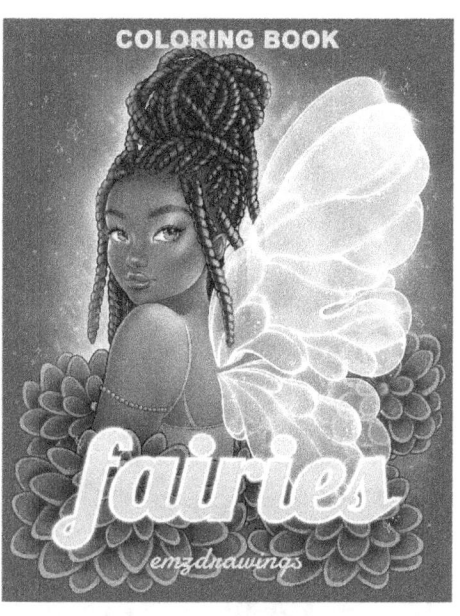

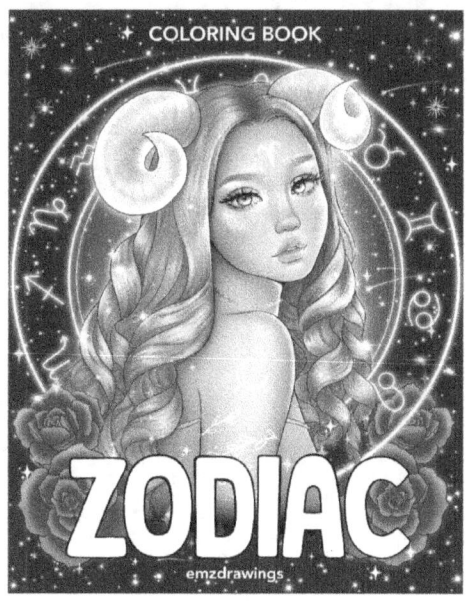

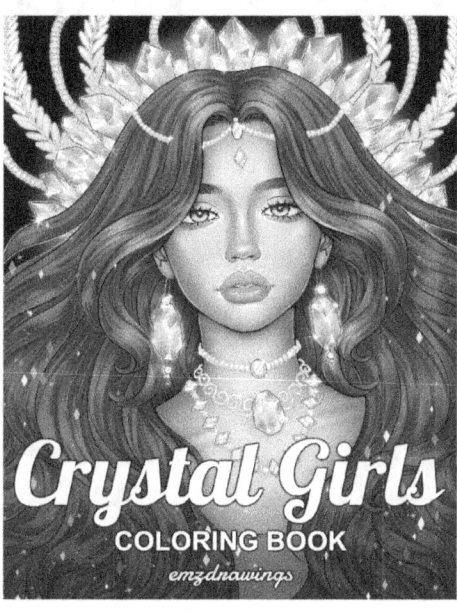

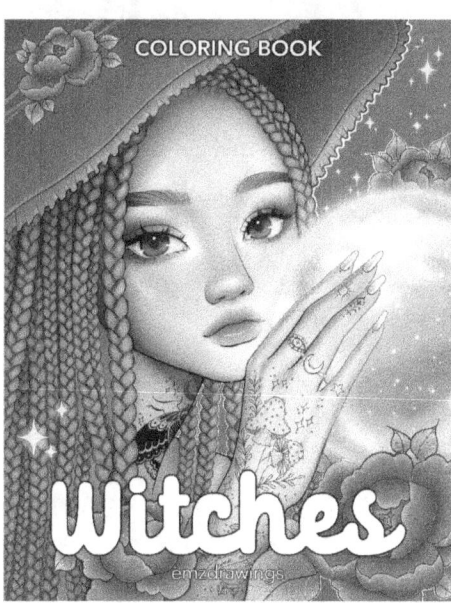